IAN R MITCHELL was born in 1947 in Aberdeen and moved in 1973 to Glasgow, where he still lives. He taught history in further education colleges for twenty-five years before taking up writing full time. Ian has written historical textbooks as well as mountaineering literature; he has received several awards, including the 1991 Boardman-Tasker Prize for Mountain Literature, for *A View from the Ridge*, co-authored wth Dave Brown; together they also wrote the bestselling classic of mountain writing, *Mountain Days & Bothy Nights*. He was awarded the 1999 Outdoor Writers' Guild Prize for *Scotland's Mountains before the Mountaineers*, a ground-breaking study which combines Ian's historical skills and mountain knowledge. His short stories have appeared in various magazines, including *Lallans, Cencrastus* and *West Coast Magazine* and in the collection *The Mountain Weeps* (1997). Ian Mitchell's grounding in history and profound grasp of mountain culture lend credibility to his first historical novel, *Mountain Outlaw*.

By the Same Author

Bismark (Holmes McDougall, 1980)
Mountain Days & Bothy Nights (Luath Press, 1988)
(with D Brown)
A View from the Ridge (The Ernest Press, 1991)
(with D Brown)
The First Munroist (The Ernest Press, 1993)
Second Man on the Rope (The Mercat Press, 1995)
Mountain Footfalls (The Mercat Press, 1996)
The Mountain Weeps (Stobcross Press, 1997)
Scotland's Mountains Before the Mountaineers (Luath Press, 1998)
On the Trail of Queen Victoria in the Highlands (Luath Press, 2000)
Walking Through Scotland's History (NMS Publishing, 2001)

Mountain Outlaw

IAN R MITCHELL

Luath Press Limited

EDINBURGH

www.luath.co.uk

First published 2003

The paper used in this book is neutral-sized and recyclable.
It is made from elemental chlorine free pulps
sourced from renewable forests.

Printed and bound by Bell & Bain Ltd., Glasgow

Typeset in 10.5 point Sabon
by Jennie Renton

To those born outside their time

Contents

Editor's Preface   ix

Bodach Caonich   1
The Officer   11
The Mother   21
The Chieftain   31
The Scientist   41
The Outlaw   53
The Laird   61
The Grazier   73
The Wife   85
The Minister   99
The Sheriff   113

Author's Afterword   125
Glossary   130

Editor's Preface

THE CHARACTER OF EWAN MACPHEE the outlaw – Eoghann Ban Coire Bhuie to give him the title he preferred – is one well known in Inverness-shire, though he has been dead for half a century, and for him it is indeed 'Lochaber no More'. There are old people yet alive who knew the bandit when they were young. His exploits are recounted and discussed to this day.

I came to these parts as a young schoolmaster, having completed my professional instruction at the Normal School in Glasgow. It was the pursuit of my leisure hours to roam the hills and glens, and in these wanderings I first came to hear of MacPhee from Hector Macmillan, a worthy old fellow known as the *bodach caonich* from his place of residing on Loch Arkaigside. In these days before the trigonometers had mapped the Highlands, he would act as my guide in forays into the wild lands between the Great Glen and the western seaboard. He was full of tales of MacPhee, many located in the area over which we walked.

I have always sustained a keen interest in this local lore and in my retirement have devoted much energy to unearthing and assembling documentary evidence of MacPhee, and this I now submit to the *Journal of the Gaelic Society of Lochaber*. Mr Macmillan's tales are also included, although I cannot vouch for their authenticity. I am keenly aware that my years are drawing to a close and I thought it useful to offer this documentation for the evaluation of others, rather than risk that it might remain unpublished in the event of my death.

I have arranged the materials in what I believe to be chronological order, rather that the order in which they came into my hands. The research has given me great pleasure. The first task I set myself was relatively easy one: since MacPhee had been arraigned for trial in Fort William in 1850, the preparatory papers would be available for public scrutiny in the legal records of the county of Inverness. I extracted the testimony of MacPhee's wife and that of his chief accuser, the grazier Cameron.

These records gave me the name of the intended presiding magistrate for the event; I therefore wrote to the descendants of the circuit judge Lord Braxburn, asking whether his papers might include a diary for the period in question. This turned out to be so, and I spent a pleasant weekend at the family home in the Borders, transcribing relevant sections.

For information on MacPhee's earlier life I searched the extensive Glengarry archive, an arduous task. I had discovered only minor references to MacPhee and his mother and was on the verge of giving up, when I came upon an unpublished letter by Sir Walter Scott and a reply from Glengarry which did much to elucidate the origins of MacPhee's controversy with his chief. One can only speculate here what the author of *Waverley* might have produced, had he based a romance on MacPhee. Presumably he accepted Glengarry's verdict on the unsuitability of the subject matter, or possibly he feared that to proceed might mean losing a friend in Glengarry. This correspondence dates from the early 1820s, when Scott and Glengarry were engaged in preparations for the visit of George IV to Scotland.

A slim pamphlet published in Oban in 1860 in memory of the

Rev Ludovick Fraser, the recently deceased minister of Kilmallie parish, provided another piece of the jigsaw: the essays in *Reflexions on Church and State* mainly concerned the Disruption of 1843, but one piece dealt with MacPhee at the time of his incarceration. This pamphlet is long out of print and I must thank the present incumbent of Kilmallie, the Rev John Mackenzie, for bringing it to my attention.

A similar act of disinterested scholarship came from an old school friend of mine, now lecturing in Geology at the University of Glasgow. At one of our annual reunions I happened to mention MacPhee. The name rang a bell and a few weeks later there appeared by the post a copy of *The Letters of Forbes McCulloch* (1883). Volume 1 contains an account of the geologist's meeting with MacPhee in 1841: this helps sketch in events following MacPhee's escape (sometime around 1820,) and his recapture thirty years later.

Mr Ellice's account of a meeting with a Glasgow bailie called MacPhee probably dates from the late 1840s. It reads rather strangely, being in the form of a monologue on Ellice's part. (Ellice purchased the Glengarry estate from the bankrupt MacDonnels.) His efforts to protect his 'adopted' bandit from retribution seem to have been based on genuine esteem. On numerous visits to Glenquoich Lodge I have received the fullest encouragement from his grandson, whose *The Place-Names of Glengarry* was recently published to considerable acclaim. He suggested that I should examine family papers at Glengarry House, where some of his grandfather's archive had been transferred. I was thrilled to find his diaries among game books and guest books, carefully stored in boxes designated year by year. Ellice kept a minute account of each day's proceedings, and had the quite original habit, when in conversation with someone of importance, of having his secretary record the dialogue in notational form, which Ellice then transcribed into his diary by his own hand.

The final document I examined was the account of MacPhee's desertion from his military service given in Volume 71 of the *War Office Papers*, (Judge Advocate General's Office, Courts Martial etc).

While the full story of Ewan MacPhee, the Robin Hood of Lochaber, may always remain as elusive as its protagonist, the documentation I have gathered, fragmentary as it is, gives a vivid picture of a charismatic character whose tragedies and triumphs were played out against a backdrop of traumatic religious and political upheaval and social transformation.

DG Place, August, 1902

Bodach Caonich

Eoghann and the *Mucan Beag*

EOGHANN MACPHEE WAS THE LAST man in Scotland to be hunted like a beast. It was Murchadh Ruadh, my father's father, who knew him, and many were the tales he told of the famous outlaw.

When Eoghann was at the wars he left his son in my grandfather's care. When he came back to the Highlands for the final time, the land was being given over to sheep. There had been much lamentation in Glen Pean and Glen Dessary when Locheil evicted the tenants; he put pressure on them to leave as if by their own will, to avoid bad words being said about him in the *Sasunnaich* newspapers.

On Locharkaigside people lost their ancient rights to graze beasts on the hillsides or collect peats. To take a rabbit, or a fish from the burn, was to risk eviction. In the cold winters they had always gathered the fallen timber that was left rotting in the felled woods. This Locheil also outlawed. The factors said the chief would pay for the emigration of those who wished it, and many there were who accepted.

But Murchadh Ruadh refused to leave the lands where his family had stayed for fifteen generations. He was a proud man. To keep up with his rents, he found work building the canal in Gleann Mor.

He gleaned fuel at night, taking the wild animals for the pot and always managed to avoid discovery, which meant instant eviction.

The clachan had only enough land round the houses for each family to have a cow and a few chickens pecking the middens – nothing more. But my grandfather had seen how the Irish labourers at the canal kept pigs which seemed to fatten up on next to nothing, so he bought a piglet from an Irishman and took it home. He let it forage on rubbish and fallen acorns in the ditch between the road and the dykes erected by the graziers to keep their sheep from straying. Everyone on the clachan saw how it got fat and what good eating it would make. Soon, even those who had spoken against bringing an unclean animal to the clachan began to talk of getting a pig. My grandfather did a small trade in the animals until one day the factor came from Locheil to tell us that the land at the side of the road belonged to the chief and any of us who used it for fattening pigs would be evicted.

There then began a hurried slaughter of pigs among the frightened tenants. But Murchadh Ruadh only said, 'Damn the pig I will get rid of for Locheil.' He defied the factor and even told him he was thinking of getting a breeding sow as well.

Sure enough, notice of eviction came to Murchadh Ruadh. The news soon reached Eoghann in his mountain hideout and he came to the clachan by night, at real risk to his life. He was the bravest man who ever lived, my grandfather said, and always true to his people in time of travail. Silently he took the eviction paper in his hand. Though he could not read, he understood well enough what it contained.

'Keep the *mucan beag*, Murchadh. And buy that sow!' he said before disappearing back into the darkness that protected him from the soldiers who were searching for him.

Later that night, the factor heard the thud of Eoghann's dirk on his door and, mistaking it for a knock, went to open it. The weapon had pinned the eviction order and a scrap of plaid into the wood. A voice came from the darkness beyond.

'That is MacPhee's dirk and MacPhee's plaid. The day you take the roof timbers from Murchadh Ruadh's house is the day you will need them to make your own coffin.'

Such was the fear in the heart of Locheil's factor that he cancelled the eviction order on Murchadh Ruadh, even claiming he had known nothing about it. He told his men to allow people to use the roadsides for their pigs. From then onwards, the clachan gained the name Muick.

Eoghann and the Pot-Still

MY GRANDFATHER TOLD ME that when Eoghann came back from fighting the French there were many stills in Lochaber. People would sell the *usquebaugh* to pay their rents, finding the labourers on the canal to be a good market. But soon after the wars, the distilleries were legalised and two were built at the Garrison. With that droves of excisemen came hunting down the illicit stills. Many were persuaded to give up the practice which brought danger and diminishing reward but Eoghann, with several stills scattered around the mountains, was further from the gaugers than most and his customers also were further from the inns, so it was worth his while to continue where others had left off. He was always careful, moved his stills around from place to place and used only oak for the fire, because it burned without smoke. When the snow fell he would stay for days with nothing to do but watch the drip, drip of *usquebaugh,* rather than allow a footprint in the snow. But all this was hard work and Eoghann was not getting any younger. People were leaving the glens and there were fewer customers to purchase his wares. One day he came and told my grandfather that he had decided to keep one still only, for the comforting of himself and his friends. However, he would play a last trick on the gaugers.

Eoghann always wore full Highland dress, fine and proudly, and he was always armed with a pair of dirks and a brace of pistols. But one day, clad in the garb of a poor cottar and without even a stick to defend himself, he went to the Garrison, to the office of the excisemen. They were *Sasunnaich* who did not know him by sight, though they had all heard of Eoghann Ban Corrie Bhuie!

Eoghann asked if there was a reward for those who reveal the place of a still.

'Aye there is, old man,' replied the chief gauger. 'Five pounds for each, or a flogging and a spell in jail, if you try to mislead us. And remember, we want the equipment, not just a place once used for the illegal trade.'

'I will show you three stills that belong to the bandit MacPhee,' was the reply.

Eoghann travelled with six well-armed gaugers to Loch Arkaig, then over into Glengarry, showing them the stills he had abandoned. The delighted gaugers smashed them and carted the debris away in knapsacks slung over their horses. Two were posted at each site in the hope of capturing the bandit himself.

When finally, Eoghann asked for his reward, the chief gauger handed him a pile of coins, asking with a sneer, 'Can you count, old man?'

'A little.'

'Oh, very good. And how many of us are there here?'
'A hundred.'
'A hundred! How do you come to that figure?'
'I'm one, and you are two nothings.'

With that, Eoghann departed, while the excisemen up in the mountains continued their futile wait for the bandit who had been with them all the time!

Eoghann and the Gamekeepers

MANY TALES THERE WERE of how Eoghann outwitted the gamekeepers, for he would never yield to an edict that ordered people to starve rather than take the animals they needed for food.

Many could not live without poaching, their condition was so bad. There were man traps in the woods, but Eoghann was always too clever to be caught in them. There were gamekeepers in the hills, armed and willing to shoot. The courts would send a man forever from his native land, if he was once caught taking one of God's animals to feed his family. Eoghann was the bold champion of the poachers. He held the chiefs and their foresters in defiance. And he did not only hunt to succour his own family. Many's the time a widow hereabouts found a haunch wrapped in a cloth tucked in the thatch of their black house by Eoghann MacPhee.

Keepers feared him. They went after the cottar poachers, rather than make a real attempt at chasing someone they could not catch. This infuriated Glengarry, who took into his employment two men from the Lowlands, promising them a great reward if they apprehended Eoghann. They lived under the protection of the laird at Invergarry itself. None would speak to them, but they seemed neither to notice nor care; indeed, they were insolent with

Glengarry's domestics and seemed more intent on feasting and drinking at their master's expense than in capturing MacPhee.

Then one day a man came to Invergarry and told that at the near end of Loch Quoich he had found the feet, head and entrails of a gralloched stag and a trail of blood in the snow where it had been dragged away. It happened to be the Sabbath, and none of Glengarry's keepers would work on the Sabbath however the factor threatened them with dismissal. But the bored Lowlanders announced they would pursue the poacher, in the hope it was MacPhee. They set off on their garrons and soon came upon the butchered stag. Even such ignorant fools as they could follow a trail of blood in the snow.

It led them to a cave whose narrow entrance was mostly obscured by a pile of rocks. The poacher must have dragged the animal into the dark space, but the keepers found there only the dead stag and no trace of MacPhee. My grandfather told me that as they came out, squeezing one at a time through the narrow cleft, MacPhee was lying in wait. He threw a sack over each of their heads, bound them up and beat them with his rifle butt until they begged for mercy.

'You will get mercy soon enough, but from your Maker,' Eoghann told the terrified pair.

He tied nooses round their necks so that if they struggled they would strangle themselves and led them by this deadly leash to the nearest clachan, a few miles down the glen. There Eoghann called out, asking if any would give the men a Christian farewell to the world. A lay preacher, an evangelical man, came forward to plead with him not to stain his hands with more blood. But when he saw the look on Eoghann's face, he said a prayer for them.

'Carry them to the edge of the clachan for burial,' ordered

Eoghann. None dared refuse him. The keepers were bound and carried on rough biers down towards the burn, beyond which lay the clachan's burial ground.

Eoghann himself took the ends of the biers and toppled the hunters turned hunted into the *poll nan con*, a deep pool below the waterfall. They thrashed around and would have surely drowned, except that some men of the clachan, moved by pity, jumped into the water and pulled the wretches out. Eoghann watched all this without motion or comment. Once the men were back on dry land he removed their hoods, saying, 'You look on MacPhee for the first time. If you see him again, it will be as your last sight on earth.'

He turned on his heel, magnificent in his fury, and was gone back to his hills.

Everyone praised Eoghann for sparing the keepers' lives, because it would have gone ill for them had two of Locheil's men been killed at their clachan. My grandfather always said Eoghann MacPhee was not the cruel fiend some people made him out to be, it was the persecution he suffered that was to blame. The days of Eoghann MacPhee and of my grandfather are long gone, and times have changed. Now we have the Land League fighting for our rights, and we could do with leaders of Eoghann MacPhee's spirit, I can tell you!

The Officer

The deposition of Major-General Mackay, made to the court martial in absentia, of Ewan MacPhee, 12th August 181—.

I WILL BE BRIEF AND TO THE POINT, as none of the matters of which I intend to speak are in dispute.

I first met the man Ewan MacPhee on the occasion of his enlistment along with several other members of the various tribes of that upland region of Lochaber called Glengarry. Some of these men I knew had been forcibly enlisted, but my sole concern was to ensure that they were all trained and equipped to the King's service to fight Bonaparte wherever the needs of warfare dictated. Their training began at Stirling Castle in the winter of 180—.

My Highland charges were such outstanding specimens, that I was convinced anew of the wisdom of enrolling the surplus population of these desert regions: possessing health and vigour which recruits from our manufacturing districts do not, and with a level of intelligence that agricultural labourers lack, the Highlanders can be shaped into excellent soldiery. Although they are without the exacting leadership qualities necessary for the higher offices of the Army, improvement in their education and society may yet rectify this deficiency.

Among these recruits, MacPhee stood out, not only by his stature and obvious strength, but by his demeanour which, though difficult to pin down as insubordination, had something haughty and arrogant in it, an attribute I had never previously observed in his compatriots. Though I kept a careful eye on him, he gave me no cause for complaint. I could see that, though doubtless incapable of commanding anything such as a regiment, he certainly commanded authority over his fellow recruits. Consequently, at the completion of his training I recommended him for promotion to the rank of corporal, a role where I felt his talents could be expressed. It was clear to me that any authority he held over his peers should be used to serve the purposes of his military superiors; unrestrained, it might work against the interests of His Majesty's forces.

Unfortunately, once the men were brought to combat readiness, we were obliged to await a theatre of war in which to prove their mettle. In barracks they talked among themselves in *Erse* so that the officers could not follow their conversation. In my experience, the Devil always makes work for idle hands, particularly among the Highlanders. I was highly impatient to depart before their training was undermined.

Stirling lies near a large coalfield which powers the Carron Iron Works, an essential sinew of our country's martial valour, by its manufacture of the Carronade military artillery. While we were awaiting our orders for departure, the miners around Stirling struck work, demanding better pay. Violence ensued: some miners who were unwilling to join the cessation of labour were burned in a vitriol attack and in retaliation one of the strikers was shot dead by an unknown assailant.

The civil magistrates then invoked the laws pertaining to workmens' combinations and declared the strike illegal; as this had no effect, appeal was made to the officer in command at Stirling to provide troops to restore order and protect those workmen who wished to go about their lawful business unmolested. The need for military intervention was perceived to be all the greater after some strikers planted a so-called Liberty Tree in the town of Fallin, at which ceremony Caps of Liberty were worn. French agents were suspected of involvement, though my own view was that local grievances were at work rather than Jacobin agents.

During this period, my recruits were given occasional leave from barracks. They used the opportunity to repair to the surrounding villages, thus becoming acquainted with the mining community and they were privy to the real or imagined grievances of the pit villages. I informed my commanding officer that it would be prudent to request troops for the purposes of maintaining order from Edinburgh or Glasgow, rather than using my raw Highland recruits. He overruled me and ordered them to present themselves, in full battle dress, ready for action. Half an hour before muster, I was given a message by my *aide de camp* that MacPhee wished to speak with me. I requested that he enter my chambers to inform me of his business.

The man stood, splendid in his military uniform, and spoke to the following effect – though I cannot reproduce his speech exactly to the letter, as I rely on memory:

'The men do not wish to fight the miners, with whom they feel they have no quarrel. The miners tell us that not ten years ago they were slaves. They have won their freedom, and now seek fair reward for their labour. My fellow recruits have taken the King's pay and are ready to fight his enemies overseas. Yet – despite my own efforts to persuade them otherwise – they wish no part in the quarrel between the miners and the authorities.'

Though he posed as a neutral *porte-parole*, I knew at once that MacPhee shared the views of his fellows. There had already been several mutinies amongst the Highland troops in Edinburgh over diverse matters, and here we were threatened with one at Stirling.

I dismissed MacPhee with the instruction that he should enjoin obedience upon the men and to await further orders. With great difficulty I persuaded my superiors to confine the Highlanders to barracks and I again requested military assistance from Glasgow. Thankfully, that very afternoon we received papers requiring us to march to a Fife port and to embark for Spain in one week's time.

Once military action was under way in the Peninsular theatre, I had no cause for complaint about MacPhee. In fact, at my instigation, he was promoted to sergeant – given his lack of education, the highest rank he could possibly achieve in the Army. I should state here that his bravery in the face of the enemy was exemplary. He was always the first of his men into action. At the siege of San Sebastian he disabled two enemy gun emplacements single-handed, for which he received decoration. However, it was in another sphere of military operations that he excelled.

When Napoleon invaded Spain, the Spaniards were forced to resort to irregular warfare of a most savage kind. Instead of engaging in direct combat, Spanish patriots attacked supply convoys, ambushed soldiery and disrupted communications. By these means they tied down surprisingly large numbers of the enemy who would otherwise have been Wellington's concern.

In these efforts MacPhee played a crucial role. His enormous strength and stamina combined with the ability, learned on his native heath, to subsist on next to nothing allowed him to be a perfect go-between for our forces and the *guerillos*. He would slip behind enemy lines on missions to contact the Spanish irregulars and pose as a gypsy, very much looking the part with his swarthy features. MacPhee would convey to our allies certain physical necessities of warfare, including money. I should mention here that at no time did MacPhee come under suspicion of dishonestly appropriating any of these materials. Unfortunately, the glamour of this clandestine role fed his vanity. He began to conceive of himself as invaluable and resented being denied what he thought was due recognition. Whilst I could, and did, strive to have him decorated for his valour and made sure he was rewarded with bounties, there was no way I could further advance his promotion; as I have already stated, the man could neither read nor write, nor had he the education in military science necessary for progress through the ranks.

During this period when MacPhee's co-operation was effectively forthcoming, my commanding officer continually chided me with partiality and with being inadequately forcible in imposing discipline over MacPhee, whose unblemished military record did not shake him from the view that MacPhee's men's behaviour at Stirling was an insolent affront to his own authority. MacPhee's voluble expression of grievance now exacerbated his irritation. My commanding officer was, I believe, looking for an opportunity to teach the Highlander a lesson.

On the occasion of which I now speak, MacPhee was sent behind enemy lines to give our Spanish allies funds for subsistence. While engaged in this task, he encountered a French patrol carrying out a search of all civilians entering the town to which he had been directed and consequently hid the coins, intending to collect them later. When circumstances prevented their immediate retrieval, he returned to camp and requested an opportunity to complete his mission. When I relayed this request to our commanding officer, I was dismissed without reply. Shortly after, he called the men out to the parade ground and addressed MacPhee as follows:

'So MacPhee, you request an opportunity to regain the money you have hidden away, doubtless against your intended desertion. Well, you Highland dog, you shall not have it. What do you say to that?'

MacPhee held his silence, staring impassively in front of him.

'You will be clapped in irons to await trial. What do you say to that?'

MacPhee refrained from speech. Taking this as an act of defiance, our superior struck a blow to the side of his face that would have flattened a man stronger than myself. MacPhee stood mute and motionless as a great tree. The commanding officer then turned on his heel, brusquely ordering MacPhee's arrest.

What followed shows that MacPhee could not endure this humiliation before his fellow Highlanders. In less time than it takes to tell of it, his dirk was drawn and plunged into the back of the commander. MacPhee had taken to his heels and disappeared over the low wall of the parade ground before any of us had the presence of mind to react. Orders for pursuit were issued, but it is my impression that these were unenthusiastically followed. MacPhee probably made for the narrow streets of the town, where he had friends and associates. He vanished completely, using the skills he formerly practised to our advantage.

In conclusion, it may be said on MacPhee's behalf that he is a man of considerable ability who believes himself the victim of injustice. However, MacPhee is a deserter from the forces of His Majesty in wartime who has murdered a superior officer: both are capital offences. The immensity of his transgressions rules out the possibility of mercy in this case.

My broader recommendation is that in order to avoid the repetition of such misfortunes, those appointed to power over Highland soldiery should be familiar with their customs and that, to this end, instruction in the particular ways of the Gael be instituted.

The Mother

Abbotsford, 12 June 18—

My Dear Mac 'ic Alasdair,

Perhaps you can furnish me with particulars of a certain Ewan MacPhee, a colourful character and romantic anachronism whose life might yet form the basis of an arresting narrative by my friend, the author of *Waverley*. I have the deepest admiration for your attempts to keep the old ways of the Gael alive. The dress, customs and sports of the Highlands, to whose survival you have devoted so much time and financial outlay, are not merely picturesque survivals of a previous epoch, but serve as symbols of loyalty for a whole nation threatened by democracy and republicanism. In this regard, the mighty charge with which I am entrusted, of bringing our gracious Majesty to Scotland, has received great inspiration from yourself.

I was ascertained of the intriguing tale of Mr MacPhee as follows. Your ghillie Sandy Vor accompanied me from Invergarry to the coach house, only to be informed that our conveyance had met with a mechanical failure at Fort Augustus and was not to be expected for several hours. The good Sandy, aware of my interest in the quaint and picturesque, and to allay the tedium, suggested a journey into the mountains, there to meet with the *cailleach Feadan*, an old crone born around the time of the last attempt to restore the Stuarts to the throne. As you might imagine, I was readily agreeable to this proposal.

We set off on ponies from the nearby inn, up a steep track that rose directly from the lochside. I must confess to some trepidation which, despite my efforts at concealment, Sandy noted with amusement. The track wound through delightful woodlands. On emerging therefrom we enjoyed magnificent vistas of the loch cradling a delicate morning mist. In an hour or so we reached a dreary pass where shivered a trio of lochans. Though I have climbed the noble peak of Helvellyn in South Britain, I confess with some shame that I had never previously ascended any of the higher peaks of North Britain. At my request, Sandy undertook to lead me to an overtowering summit whose Gaelic name means the Hill of the Tongue. After hobbling our mounts, we proceeded through a rough boulder-field and soon sat on the summit beside a cairn which Sandy himself had built while deer-watching there for the guests of the estate. The view south down the Great Glen extended to the snow-streaked crags of Ben Nevis. 'All you can see is Glengarry's,' Sandy boasted, adding with poetic licence, 'and all you cannot see, that is Glengarry's too!'

We fell silent, awed by the splendour of the scene, before returning to our mounts to descend into a pleasant upland champaigne, where we arrived at the door of a solitary habitation. Its occupant awaited us at the portal. I noticed instantly that she was blind. However, I was not surprised at her awareness of our approach for, as I have often observed, the loss of one faculty often causes others to grow more acute: the old woman evidently had a highly developed sense of hearing. She and Sandy exchanged greetings in Gaelic and we were invited to enter the crude dwelling, which she apparently maintained almost entirely by her own efforts.

Having conveyed her willingness to tell me her life story, *cailleach Feadan* then commenced to sing in a low, monotonous, yet pleasant voice, apparently composing extempore; Sandy obliged with a translation. As always, I had my pocket book with me and took down as much as I could.

I am assured that the metrical and rhyming schemes of the Gael in poesy are complex but I have made no attempt to reproduce these in my transcription, a literal rendition, which I append, in all its roughness, to this letter. I am disposed to hope, my dear Mac 'ic Alasdair, that you have further intelligence concerning this woman's son, whose escapades took place in part on your ancestral homelands.

I offered the good woman some trifling coin for her narration. This she refused, asking only that I put in a word for her son with the 'great ones', mentioning yourself in particular, and this request I now honour. I fully understand that her son is a deserter deserving the full rigours of the law. However, now that hostilities are over, is it not possible to offer amnesty, if he give himself up to the authorities?

The hour is late and I must draw this correspondence to a close. My mind is preoccupied with the state of the populace in our towns: there are credible rumours of plans for seditious rebellion. In Selkirk, the soutars have attacked and stoned the civil magistrates. How happy, in these troubled times, to be as you are, the clan chief of a populace still bound to you by traditional bonds!

Ever your truly obliged and faithful
Walter Scott (Bart.)

The Mother's Lament

He was born in an evil hour, as was I myself.
The Year of the Prince saw my birth,
The Year of the Return saw the return of my son.
Cameron and Clan Ranald regained possession

No more did we pay rent to chiefs abroad
Or to the sassunaich Commissioners
Men said in expectation of ancient ways,
'There will be raiding in Lochaber once more.'

But the chiefs to a man forgot their ancestors.
Clarsach and pibroch sounded no more
The halls of Invergarry and Achnacarry
Rang to the chatter of strangers.

The ways of the Gall they brought with them.
Though they might wear the plaid and the dirk
They felled the trees fringing the lochs
And scarred the braes with quarries and mines.

To those burdened with two rents of forty summers
They brought no message of gratitude
But only word that they must pay or
Be winnowed from the land of twenty generations.

In the late summer of that year
In the late summer of my childbearing

Thinking myself far past fecundity
Eoghann was born to me.

The blessing of a son we accepted
As we had accepted the chiefs' return.
The sorrow at both came later
Though the one of them was not intended.

Eoghann sprung of courageous seed
Fine as Locheil and MacDonnel
Who had burned to death in their strongholds
Or bitten out the throats of the soldiers of Cromwell.

MacPhees had fought for the royal Stuarts
With the gallant Montrose and the stalwart Dundee
They were no strangers to Sheriffmuir
Unlike the Campbells who fought for usurping Hanover.

Locheil said any man leaving sword in thatch
Would have the thatch burned over his head.
MacDonnel sent one to fight for the Prince
But another stayed at home for the usurper.

There was no such hesitation from the man
Who was my son's father.
With the others who had lifted their swords
He planted a stick to mark the numbers leaving.

Having courage and fearing no hardship
He fared into the lands of the Prince's enemies.

The speech of the Saxon brought him no joy
The clash of battle was music to his ears.

At Eaclaisbhric and at Drumossie Moor
While weaker men deserted the standard
He was the last to leave the battlefield
As the red soldiers began their butchery.

At the pass of Fedden half the sticks had no claimants
And though my husband reclaimed his sorrowfully
He was forced into hiding, as far as the Rough Bounds,
While the soldiery burned through the glens.

A man among the Cleansers had a hard heart.
If you would not forswear the Prince and chiefs
Munro burned the houses and killed the cattle
As far as Glean Pean and Glen Dessary.

But fortune did not always smile on him.
A shot was heard in the Dark Mile,
And Culcairn of the white horse and black heart died.
Fortune smiled on the deed of my husband.

The Prince boarded a ship to France
And like all things the Cleansing passed.
New men came to the lands of Cameron and Clan Ranald
Though we would not forswear allegiance to the chiefs.

The new men were in truth not ill-meaning
But they knew not the ways of the glens.

With another language we wanted no dealings
Nor with their ideas of alteration.

To a man advanced in years one son was born.
Worn out by his labours in Strontian
Mining for lead in the cold bowels of the earth
He had to work to pay commissioners and chief.

More like a grandfather than a father
He told of Drumossie Moor and Culcairn
And of the ancient freedom of the Gael
Before he went to rest in ancestors' earth.

There was myself alone to raise the boy
Bold and free, like one of the Fianna,
On the slopes of Coire Bhuie under Sgurr Mor
His shouts and laughter would resound.

Hardship there was at Fedden
For a widow helped by neighbours
Till Ewan grew unto fine manhood
And took in the harvest with his own lads.

Happy were the days at Fedden
Of a mother and her son,
Till the day the factor came
And there was no money for rent.

In the time of war with the French
In a place far away called Spain

Ewan must go with the Fencibles
Unless he wished his mother without a roof.

Ten years I did not see him
Though stories were told of his valour.
Then he crossed my hearth as fugitive
Pursued like the deer on the mountains.

The days of the Gael are gone.
Everywhere is the hour of the Saxons.
No longer do the mountains offer sanctuary
As they did before the coming of the Prince.

Now by my house there is close watch.
I fear to touch Eoghann no more.
An old woman weeps at Fedden
For a son under sentence of death.

The Chieftain

Invergarry, 15th August, 18—

Dear Friend,

As ever, it was a pleasure to hear from you. Please convey my best regards to the author of *Waverley*, that 'Wizard of the North' with whom you are closer acquainted than most, and also to Lady Scott. I trust the ancient hospitality of the Gael will always be yours to enjoy, on your too-infrequent visits north to out humble home.

Your encounter with Mrs MacPhee had much of the romantic about it, which I know appeals to your imagination. That you were well pleased with your meeting I heard from Sandy, who indicated that he was rewarded liberally for guiding you to the old woman at Fedden.

You request further details of the MacPhees and I am happy to oblige, though what I have to convey is not of a romantic nature, unlike the song of the *cailleach,* which bears little relation to the truth. The events I relate, while more prosaic, will make clear why it is not possible for me to bring any influence to bear upon the matter of clemency for MacPhee, whose deeds are of such an atrocious nature that, even were his previous misdemeanours forgiven, he could still expect nothing but the gallows.

MacPhee's family sprang originally from Loch Arkaigside in the lands of Cameron of Locheil. His father was born sometime betwixt the two ill-fated attempts last century to restore the Stuart family to the throne. The MacPhees had traditionally been given to banditry, preying mainly on drovers. One especially dreadful incident concerns the offer they made to escort a party of Lowland cattlemen to Loch Quoich. Acting with apparent favour, the MacPhees led the drovers into a massacre, afterwards throwing them into the loch. Their bodies floated downstream and some of the local populace buried them – the burial mound can still be seen at the foot of Loch Quoich.

MacPhee's father, Eoghann Dubh – Black Ewan – was apprenticed early to lawlessness, but the Year of the Prince intervened. Eoghann Dubh needed no encouragement to join the levies which were being raised by Locheil – probably he was motivated more by the prospect of plunder rather than by political loyalty to the House of Stuart. He deserted the Jacobite army after the Battle of Prestonpans and returned home with his bounty and so he was not part of the advance into England. But he rejoined the force at the Battle of Falkirk, ultimately fleeing with his life from the moor at Culloden.

After the destruction of Jacobite hopes, Eoghann Dubh returned to the shores of Loch Arkaig. All sorts of stories circulated about him. Certainly he resumed his banditry. Some said he had Locheil's protection and that he helped organise that unfortunate chief's escape abroad. Your *cailleach* attributes to him the assassination of Munro of Culcairn. You should know, Sir, there are as many claimants to that celebrated deed as a cat has lives.

Eoghann Dubh took for his wife the woman you recently encountered. While active persecution of former insurgents was a thing of the past, soldiery was still billeted in the glens to discourage banditry. The Forfeit Commissioners ran Highland estates firmly and tenants were expected to pay their rent, on pain of eviction. The MacPhees had never paid rent to Locheil when he was in residence and most certainly did not pay him when he was in exile, despite what the good woman at Fedden informed you. However, to meet the Commissioners' demands, Eoghann Dubh took employment in the lead mines at Strontian, which were prospering passably well in the more settled times since 1745. No doubt using the native charm of the Gael, he soon became popular and trusted. But the charm of this particular Gael was no more than a crafty mask. He ambushed the paymaster on his way to the mines, cut his throat in cold blood and fled with the money. There were no witnesses to the attack and probably not enough proof to stand up in a court of law, but the fact that Eoghann Dubh never showed his face again at the mines was highly suggestive and the general consensus was that he was guilty.

After the incident at Strontian, Eoghann Dubh apparently built a house at Corrie Bhuie on the shores of Loch Quoich. Though he and his wife were both fairly advanced in years a son was born. About five years later, Eoghann Dubh died. Bereft of the means of support, his wife shifted to Fedden to be closer to her relatives and took over an abandoned steading for her home. (Incidentally, Fedden is from a Gaelic word meaning the chanter of the bagpipe because of the noise made by the wind howling through the pass.) She initially subsisted on charity – indeed the tenantry hereabouts will let no one starve while they have as much as a crust to share.

There is no need to acquaint you with the difficulties which the house of Glengarry has experienced in the years since the return of the forfeited estates and the Government amnesty for former

Jacobite supporters. Our estate is so heavily encumbered with debt that we find ourselves hard pressed to maintain the circumstances befitting one of the oldest families in the kingdom. Maintaining a presence in Edinburgh and London, as one is now obliged to do, is an additional burden. The tenantry protested loyalty to me but were obdurately resistant to paying the rent the estate requires to keep up with necessary outgoings. Inured in their indolent ways, some protested inability to pay, others sullenly asserted that the land belonged to the clan and not the chief. I had no option but to evict such malcontents so that I might lease my lands for a reasonable return.

The boundary between the lands of my house and those of Locheil lies at the Fedden watershed, a marshy area whence issues a burn. It had been somewhat indeterminate, and contested for many years. Hearing that a woman and her child now occupied an abandoned hovel there, my factor went to demand rent. She haughtily refused, claiming that she was not on Glengarry land. She gave the identical to Locheil's factor. As long as neither Glegarry nor Locheil had legal title to the lands it was impossible to pursue the case and so she lived there for many years rent free. Eventually the Court of Session awarded me title to the disputed territory and I set about eliminating this anomalous situation. I stand by the principle that one cannot make exceptions, not least because exceptions set examples. One cannot expect some tenants to pay their rent while others leech upon one's liberality. Accordingly, I instructed my factor to visit the *cailleach Feadan*, as she was known, to inform her that I was willing to allow her to remain in residence, provided she pay rent. I was prepared to forgo the back rent due, on condition that her son, by now a vigorous lad, enter the armed forces. His pay would be diverted directly to me and the surplus forwarded to her, so that she need not be concerned with the transaction. My factor made it clear that refusal would cause me to enforce eviction. No doubt out of consideration for his old mother, Ewan went with off to the Peninsular War and by all accounts acquitted himself well in battle, gaining a modest promotion. Three years later he was demobilised and returned to these parts, full of arrogance and with money in his pocket. He spent it entertaining cronies in local hostelries. A local woman bore him a son. She died in childbirth. It is said that MacPhee had administered a concoction prepared from clubmoss, intending to produce a termination. Though the fluxions it induces may result in death, such means are not uncommonly resorted to. However, MacPhee's child survived and he provided funds for it to be boarded out.

MacPhee claimed to have the second sight and he made a modest income out of uttering prophesies to the credulous peasants. I am informed that a small coin would produce a bad omen for its giver. He claimed a *bocan* had appeared to him in the form of a huge dog at the siege of San Sebastian. The ghost reputedly told him to fear nothing, as he would return home safely from the wars – which, to the curious logic of his hearers, was proof that MacPhee's vision had occurred. MacPhee began to embroider on these tales, saying that every night, after he left the inn, the *bocan* would challenge him to a fight which sometimes lasted till the crowing of the cock at dawn led to the apparition's disappearance. If MacPhee won, the ghost would issue him further prophesies. The superstitious took this nonsense as further proof of MacPhee's powers, rather than evidence of a brain disordered by a fevered imagination and excess of alcohol.

Matters came to a head when I was informed that MacPhee, moved by a chronic sense of grievance, had begun uttering prophesies prejudicial to the house of Glengarry. I had MacPhee summoned to an audience with me at Invergarry. His lack of respect manifested itself in his answer: he could not come on the appointed day, but would come the day following. To avoid having to remove his hat in my presence, he already held it in his hands as he entered. I asked him to recount the prophesies he had been making concerning my family.

'It is not myself who foretells what is to come, but the *bocan*,' he replied. 'The *bocan* says that I will come through all dangers whether in the *Gaidhealtachd* or in the world of the *Sasunnach* and that I will eventually lie buried in the lands of Glengarry.'

He told me that I would not wish to hear what the ghost had said of Glengarry, but I insisted.

'The *bocan* says you will be the last of the Glengarry chiefs, for you have forsworn the old ways. After your death, which will come in a terrible accident, the lands will go from the MacDonnels.'

I know such superstitions are rubbish, but I also knew my tenantry. The way they would see it, if Glengarry's time was limited, what need for loyalty and obedience, what need to pay rent, what need to submit to eviction? Seditious rumour-making could not be allowed. Accordingly, I conveyed to MacPhee via my factor that I would give him a sum of money if re-enlisted as a soldier. I admit I was surprised at how easily he assented. Had he perhaps become bored with life in time of peace? Whatever the case, I thought myself rid of the fellow and his predictions.

Nothing was seen of MacPhee in Lochaber for many years. Regular remittances would arrive at my factor's office, with a note 'To the account of the widow at Fedden'; it could not have been in MacPhee's hand, for he is illiterate. This covered her rent and allowed a moderate surplus for her other needs. The payments abruptly stopped, followed by the news that MacPhee had deserted his colours after a murderous dispute with a superior officer.

Like a salmon returning to the stream of its birth, he traversed the continent and returned to Lochaber, with a sentence of death now hanging over him. From his mother's account, he visited her before disappearing into the wilds. In the intervening years since then, the happy events at Waterloo have finally put an end to Napoleon's attempts to deliver Europe into the hands of republicanism.

I must tell you that since MacPhee's return there has been a series of atrocious incidents throughout Lochaber attributed to him. These include everything from murder and violent robbery to the violation of women. Even if he can honestly plead not guilty to some of these crimes, it is certain that others were committed at his hand. MacPhee is generally sly and leaves no witnesses to his evil deeds but recently one has come forward who is prepared to swear that the murder of a peddlar in the Dark Mile was by MacPhee's hand. A warrant for his arrest has been issued.

Events have gone too far for the mercy of the law to be appealed to. I would be guilty of neglect of duty were I to intercede. I have already done him too many favours and his notorious example is pernicious in these times of uncertainty. However colourful his character may seem, MacPhee's glamour is skin deep and he would certainly not be a suitable subject for the author of *Waverley*. The works of that master call upon us to admire the chivalric traditions of the Gael, whose noble traits MacPhee utterly lacks. Ewan MacPhee is not Rob Roy. His presence in Lochaber threatens my efforts to strengthen the bond of ancient loyalty between chief and people, a bond that is threatened by the spirit of this age. MacPhee has much in him of the 'democratic' insubordination so prevalent in these unhappy times. When he is eventually apprehended, I will be gratified to assist his removal in chains from these parts, to serve trial at the High Court, where he will receive his just deserts.

His mother, however, may live out her remaining days at Fedden. I give you my word on that.

I hope the above does not disappoint you overmuch and assure you that I remain your ever faithful friend and admirer,

Glengarry

The Scientist

My dear James,

As you are my closest scientific colleague, I enclose for your critical comments, before I submit it to the editor of the *Philosophical Journal*, my draft paper on 'The Topography and Geology of the Rough Bounds of Knoydart'.

Amidst the splendid formation of these mountains are indisputable traces of glaciers, offering labourers in the vineyard of science arguments against Creationist and Vulcanist theories. The struggle for political reform and the advancement of the working classes in which we are both engaged is best served by the construction of a rational world outlook. The fight against Old Corruption was only begun with the passing of the Great Reform Bill. I am certain you will be as excited as I am by the news from the manufacturing districts as to the progress of the Charter, and the resolution evinced by the workmen to pursue their cause to a successful conclusion, by moral force if possible, or by physical force if needs be!

I also forward some information which you will find rewards study. These observations concern a man who has been, in a manner of speaking, my co-worker in the field over the last few months.

He is the most amazing character. He has led a life which seems utterly anachronistic in this modern age. Science and industry are progressing with astonishing rapidity, reformers like Mr Owen are formulating rational plans for the co-operation and happiness of humanity, yet in the Highlands of Scotland, a mere railway journey away, I encountered this extraordinary fellow, some sort of bandit, whose tales of injustice and deprivation belong more to the days of priestly superstition and feudal oppression.

I will proceed to my first encounter. As you know, the area I have been studying is of great geological interest. I had been a couple of weeks in the field, making notes and sketches and taking rock samples. I am blessed with a robust constitution and as the weather was fair, I slept out in the heather, wrapped in a plaid. I drank of the sweet mountain water and consumed the frugal provisions with which I had burdened my sheltie before leaving Fort William. Of an evening I occasionally caught a burn trout, to vary my fare. The wildness of these parts cannot be exaggerated. Apart from the sight of an occasional shepherd on a distant hill, I had met no other person. But someone had discerned me, as I was to discover.

I had been on a mountain called *Sgurr na Ciche*, a majestic declivity which reminds me of some of the mountains in the Valais, or in Savoy. The summit was pre-eminent amongst the neighbouring peaks and from it I hoped to produce a sketch-map of the topography of the region. With my sketch book in my wallet and some specimens of rock chosen more for their beauty than for any scientific interest, I was returning to camp through a glen so desolate that, even before the recent clearance of the population from this area, no soul could have subsisted there. I was so intent on my philosophical musings, that I almost bumped into MacPhee, where he stood on the faint track. He shouted a warning, drawing my attention to the rifle which he pointed straight at me. I stopped, tried to compose myself, and asked him his business (which I hoped was robbery, rather than murder – he was of massive proportions and I could not have hoped to engage successfully with him in any physical combat.)

'It is *your* business that I am enquiring after,' he stated in the brogue of a Highlander unused to the English language. 'I have been watching you for some days now, wandering the mountains, writing things in that book you have. You are not a hunter, though you sometimes take a fish. You tend no still, nor do you herd any animals. You are now in the lands of Ewan MacPhee, where no man passes without my leave. Explain yourself and show me what is written in your book, or it will go ill with you.'

He evidently suspected me of evil intent. I deduced from his anxiety about my note-taking that he was being pursued by the law. If so, it was imperative that I convince him my presence was innocent of threat. With elaborate deference I replied, 'Mr MacPhee, I regret if I have been in these parts without paying you my respects. However, I was unaware that anyone lived in these mountains. My error was not intentional. Surely it is not the way of the Gael to welcome a stranger with a deadly weapon, but rather with hospitality? If you please, lay aside your weapon and I will explain. You need no rifle, for as you can see, I am unarmed and would be unable to offer you opposition in combat.'

This reference to his strength seemed to please him. I think also he felt the charge of lack of hospitality, always a sensitive point with these people. As I held out my notebook for his inspection, he laid aside his rifle to accept my offering. Naturally he could not read, though he pretended that he could follow my jottings, which are unintelligible to any but myself. I did not offer to aid him, knowing that he would be offended. Even the rudest peasant here is sensitive of his dignity to an inordinate degree. I waited for him to enquire further as to my purpose. His deduction as to my activities astonished me.

'You are an artist of some kind?' he enquired.

'How do you form that impression, Mr MacPhee?'

'You make drawings of the mountains in your book. Some of those who come to Glenquoich to stay with the laird make drawings of the mountains. Sometimes they draw me as well,' he said with a note of pride.

'I can assure you that I am no artist, despite these sketches. I am a geologist. I study the rocks of the earth, their composition and formation. The notes are my observations on the rocks of this area, while the sketches show the structure of the more notable mountains.'

MacPhee silently considered my comments. He studied my notebook. Then he pointed to my most recent sketch, observing that it was a portrait of the mountain whose name I gave earlier: *Sgurr na Ciche.* MacPhee now appeared less suspicious towards me and I seized the initiative by asking him to look at other sketches and to give me the names of those peaks. This task delighted him. There was not a single mountain whose name he did not know, as well as the meaning of that name in the Gaelic tongue. I asked his leave to write down what he was telling me as best I could in my crude Erse. This he granted. Then he noticed the sketch I had most recently made and asked which mountain it represented. I told him it was a map of the whole area. Curiously, he seemed unable to grasp this idea; his mind worked on a practical pictorial level, but apparently he could not follow an abstraction of this nature.

However, our discussions appeared to have established a basis of trust. We became colleagues, in a manner of speaking.

MacPhee was satisfied with my explanations as to my presence and conveyed that he wished me no ill; in fact, while I was in the region I could rest assured that he would protect me, he said. Though I felt in the need of such protection only from MacPhee himself, I thanked him heartily, as he obviously expected me to. He then took his departure, assuring me that he would return the next day, at the same hour. I milled over the episode all evening, wondering as to the history of this wild man who was clearly some sort of miscreant evading the ministrations of the law.

On the following evening he returned to my camp. He expressed himself pleased with my abilities to sustain the rigours of life in the mountains, and praised my pedestrian abilities, which he had been observing unbeknownst to me. He had brought the liver of a deer which he had killed, saying that it was proper food for a man, and a clay vessel of whisky of his own brewing, which he offered as a gift for my own usage. I invited him to share my repast and he took a seat, or rather, squatted, beside my fire. His circumstances may have limited his education, but a lively curiosity expressed itself in the questions he posed to me. How did I manage to live, when I spent my time drawing mountains and chipping rocks? When I told him it was my employment, and that I was a teacher at a kind of school – for he had no concept of university – he was amazed that money could be deployed by the authorities to subsidise such frivolity. Pressed as to the usefulness of my work, I informed him that it told how the earth was formed and allowed us to locate deposits of precious minerals. He argued that asking local people such as himself would lead to quicker discoveries, as they knew where such riches as iron and lead were to be found in the rocks.

He looked sceptical when I asserted that to locate the deeper and more valuable deposits, the application of learning was required. Contradiction caused him to retreat into himself. I realised that I would learn more of his life if I maintained the role of occasional questioner.

In the days following I had pleasant and useful conversations with MacPhee, who seemed to have plenty of time at his disposal. Recalling his initial suspicion of me and the likelihood of his illegal proclivities, I was careful never to enquire as to his calling. He would tell me in good time, if he so chose. However, I realised that if I had him as a field worker, I would be able to undertake my work more efficaciously. The Gael still takes it as a considerable insult to be offered hired labour, which is seen as a badge of servitude. In the case of my sensitive host, I needed to phrase the offer carefully.

One evening we were taking a dram when MacPhee came across one of my drawings of the buckling and folding of the earth under the pressures of its formation. He surprised me by observing that this was a formation he was familiar with and that it lay on a mountain towards Loch Hourn. In this assertion he was correct. I asked him if he knew of any similar formations and he stated that, yes, indeed he did. I tried him with another sketch, of glacier markings on the rocks at the outlet of a lochan. Again, such scars were familiar to him from other locations in his mountain domain. I seized the moment.

'Mr MacPhee,' – for such I was always careful to call him – 'my work is burdensome and I have no helper. Your knowledge of these hills is unique and I would be honoured if you could help me in locating geological formations and aiding me with the general work of my expedition. At its completion, you can put the value on your assistance that you deem fit and fair.'

MacPhee perceived my proposal as an honour, since I had put myself in a position of supplicant and he was keen for the chance to show off his expertise. He assented, and for the next two weeks we were inseparable. He tended the sheltie and assured our supplies through hunting and fishing. At night he would prepare a primitive nomad's shelter, though we continued to be blessed by good weather. I do not wish to convey that he was merely a factotum beguiled into service by flattery. Show the man an example of sedimentary formation in a sketch, and he could take you to a similar example in the mountains. Though his scientific knowledge was non-existent, his eye was astonishingly acute.

I discovered that he reckoned by no Julian or other calendar. To him the past was simply a succession of years, some of which were exceptional enough to have a name, such as the Year of Waterloo. He was uncertain of his own age, though he thought himself to be upwards of fifty. He might be the only man to think Bishop Ussher's estimate of our planet's lifetime as too long, rather than too short. I do not think he could conceive of a time span of six thousand years. He dismissed scientific curiosity as an attribute of a spoilt child.

Other talents of this primitive were equally astounding. I am, as you know, no sloth as a pedestrian; I can out-walk most people. However, the speed and stamina of MacPhee on the hill was more like that of an animal than a man, despite his youth being at some distance past. His low, crouching gait subjected me to a pace I could not often maintain.

I asked him if there were any extinct volcanoes in his territory, showing him the shape of a volcano in a drawing. He took me to a mountain which he thought might fit the description, but my desire to scale it was moderated by the sight of a steep and slippery snow field which had outlasted the summer, guarding access to the summit.

I have resorted to some desperate measures in my geological explorations. I once used my mahogany tripod as an extra leg to negotiate the crevasses on an Alpine glacier and you will recall how we have descended rocky faces on the mountains of Skye by using your scarf as a rope. However, I could see no way of egress from our difficulty by proceeding, and proposed retreat to my fellow geologist. He laughed at my weakness with his usual indulgence and produced two dirks from somewhere inside his plaid, which seemed to contain all manner of items within its folds. MacPhee always went barefoot, the horn on his feet was like leather. As I watched, he used his dirks as purchase to lever himself up the slope, inserting his feet in the small cavities made by the points of the weapon and enlarging the hollows as he ascended. In seconds he was at the summit, calling upon me to follow. I knew I must ascend, or lose face with my companion. My task was made easier by the disturbance of the snow which MacPhee had already effected, but it was with much disquiet that I imitated his advance. However, it was with an extraordinary sense of euphoria that I eventually stood beside him on the summit of the extinct volcano.

MacPhee's political opinions are as you might expect. There are points of contact with someone like myself, but few. He hates the landlord class, not from any understanding of their parasitic and superannuated nature, but simply because some of their number have done him real or imagined injustices. He has some sympathy with the plight of the working classes, telling me that as a young soldier he became familiar with the miners of the Lowlands, whom he considers a fine set of people, treated as badly by their employers as the peasantry hereabouts are by their landlords. A description of the political system which now obtains in this country seems as difficult for him to comprehend as the history of the formation of the earth. The Six Points of the Charter which I elaborated to him one night, he simply could not relate to his own existence, saying only that it was not possible to chose a chief (for as such he construes our parliamentarians), but only to choose to obey or disobey him, if he be good or bad. 'A man can survive anything with strength and courage,' is his credo.

The time of my acquaintance with this remarkable character was drawing to a close, yet I still had not drawn him concerning his own affairs, beyond occasional reference to slights he had suffered in the Army into which he was pressed at the time of the wars against Revolutionary France. However, I informed him one night that this would be our last together, whereupon I offered him five sovereigns, as his help had indeed been very beneficial to my scientific work. With great dignity he took but three of the coins offered, saying that was, in his estimation, the value of his time expended in my service. There was unease in his demeanour, which I put down to regret at our parting. We really had been ideal companions. However, the cause of his disquiet lay elsewhere.

'I have sat by your fire and enjoyed your hospitality,' he observed, 'and I am ashamed that, though I have brought offerings to your table, I have not invited you to my hearth. But I cannot.'

'Why not, if I may ask?' was my quietly spoken response. I sensed a wish from him that I should ask, that he might explain.

'No man must know where Ewan MacPhee resides. No man, not even yourself,' he uttered in typically grandiloquent manner. I repeated my question. I listened to his answer almost without moving, allowing the fire to burn down unattended. I later transcribed his tragic tale as far as I could from memory. While I am obviously unable to comment as to the veracity of his narrative, it had an epic quality in its telling, to which I cannot hope to do justice.

I look forward to your comments on my scientific paper, and to our renewal as brothers in arms in the struggle for the Charter and the co-operative commonwealth, in which we will fight like a pair of Ewan MacPhees. Whatever sins the man has committed, his determination to struggle for justice as he sees it is a quality which demands admiration.

With my best regards,

Forbes MacCulloch

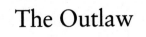

The Outlaw

I LEFT THE ARMY OF MY OWN WILL, as was my right, since I had been forced to enlist against my will. I was hiding near Loch Arkaig when I heard the wars were over. I thought the pursuit would slacken and travelled with less caution. But I was betrayed by a peddlar. Soldiers from the Garrison came and took me to Corpach, chained like a beast. The crowd jeered at them as I was taken aboard the Devil's engine, which was moored at the pier, its funnel belching black smoke. A blacksmith was brought to fasten my manacles to an iron ring on the deck, but John Balgowan was known to me and as he left he said under his breath, 'It will not hold, Ewan, it will not hold your flight. I can do no more for you than that.'

John had spoken true, the iron ring would not have held a dog. The boat had to turn before it headed out across the loch. I took my chance when the back of the steamer was at its closest to the pier, and took a mighty leap. The hands of my brothers and sisters pulled me to freedom, enclosing me in their midst. The soldiers, who were all positioned on the prow, only noticed my escape when it was too late. To much rejoicing, John the smith struck off my shackles and hurled them into the waters of the loch. Though my feet and wrists were sorely cut and grazed, the firing behind me made me run like a goat over the braes of Locheilside. I made for my mother's house. She would give me her sheltie to aid my flight. That was to be the last time I ever saw my dear, blind mother, though I did not know it at the time. I went straight after to the house of the peddlar, and killed the traitor.

I travelled through the emptiness of Glen Kingie and over the mountains to Lochan nam Breac. Shepherds go there now, but this was before the coming of the sheep. I dismissed the sheltie, which I knew would find its way back to Fedden. I found a hollow against a cliff, sheltered by some fallen boulders with a small burn trickling across the sandy floor for drinking water within my place of concealment. There were some fallen and dead trees, birch and rowan among the rocks. I would only light a fire on days when the mist was deep enough to hide the smoke. Most days I did without. I roofed my shelter with branches and greenery, though it was but poor protection against the weather. With the hunger and cold came wicked dreams, night after night. Dreams of the peddlar screaming for mercy, dreams of the horrors of San Sebastian. I thought I would go mad.

Then the *bocan* came to me. He told me I would outlive Glengarry and all my persecutors. Then the very next day I heard a commotion and on venturing cautiously out, saw the biggest *erne* I had ever seen, swooping down at a wounded stag on the cliff top. One of the stag's legs hung useless, otherwise it would never have been attacked like that. The beast could not flee its screeching persecutor and it was driven back to the edge of the cliff. Suddenly it fell full over, smashing on the rocks in front of my shelter. I looked up but the *erne* was nowhere to be seen in the clear skies. I knew then that it was really the *bocan*, come to help me in the form of an eagle.

I dragged the broken stag across the rocks and for the rest of the winter I ate my way through the broken beast. Buzzards came by day and foxes by night to feed on the carrion, but my alertness left them with the smaller part. In the worst of the winter the corpse froze solid, and then I would suck at the cold meat for sustenance. When it was soft, I ate it raw. Once or twice I cooked slices of the liver over a stealthy fire. I ate the eyes and the brain, I sucked the marrow from the bones and, towards the end, I swallowed the fattened maggots which fell from the rotting skin and the bones.

When only a skeleton lay on my roof, with strips of skin from which I had sucked all nourishment hanging in tatters, the spring began to come. With the melting of the snow came the *bocan* once more, to let me know it was safe to come out of hiding.

The hunt had slackened off, but there was still a price on my head. I risked forays to get supplies but I let no one know where I was dwelling.

For many years I lived in the mountains like the deer and the fox, before I came to my present habitation. It came to my ears that Glengarry had been killed by an explosion on the Devil's Engine, the very boat which had been intended for my transportation. The *bocan*'s prediction was fulfilled.

There is one thing I cannot forget. I have told no living soul of this but as the sun rises it fills my mind and as the sun sets it fills my dreams. Hard as all these times were the hardest was yet to come.

I had two sons and two daughters. My second son was borne away by the *tarbh-uisge*. Long before I met my wife Helen, another woman bore me the first boy. She died in the bearing of him. I was not able to care for him, so he was fostered with a family from Glen Dessary and I never knew the boy, though I heard he grew up well enough. The people of the glens were suffering, there were many evictions and there was hunger. I sometimes bartered meat against my own small needs. This meant trips down to the glens, which I made always at night and fully armed. When it was safe enough I would met friends at the local inn where we would share tales and I could sell charms and potions to pay for my revelry.

One night I was at Caonich delivering some venison to a cottar, who told me that the new man in charge at the Garrison had increased the reward on my head and put fresh patrols in the glens. There were soldiers at the inn and I should avoid it that night, he told me. I was angered, angered that old scores would not be let to rest and that I was excluded from the companionship of my fellows.

Every crime in Lochaber is lodged against Ewan MacPhee. If it is true that I rob the people, why do they protect me? Why do they refuse to betray me, as their ancestors refused to betray the Prince? I take only what the country produces. How can the lairds own the wild beasts? They are no more able to own the wind and the water, than animals they have neither bred nor fed.

I headed back up the mountain in a bitter mood, but soon became aware that I was being followed. I can see a deer at a distance none other can, I can hear and smell them. I can tell by the ground how many people have gone there and how they were shod. I always return back on my path if I am being followed, but this time there was no need. I could clearly hear the footfall of my pursuer on the twigs and leaves. When I emerged from the wood onto the moor I hid behind a stone, till I saw a solitary figure leaving the wood. I leapt out at my pursuer and challenged him. He told me he was seeking Ewan MacPhee but I was sure he was out to betray me and in my anger I seized the youth, drew a pistol and gave him a whipping about the head, telling him to leave Ewan MacPhee alone, and let others know to do the same. But when I released him from my grip, the manner of his falling was that of a dead man. I swear I had no intention to kill him. But the deed was done, so I made it seem that he had died in a fall. From that day to this, suspicion has never fallen on me. But when I next visited the clachan I realised from the talk that I had killed my own son.

I have been falsely accused of legions of crimes, and I refute those accusations. Yet none but me knows of this terrible sin, that I murdered my firstborn son. In my heart there is emptiness. They say I am brave. But I do not have the courage to tell them this. I can tell this to you because we have shared knowledge together and soon you will leave these parts forever, to return to a world which knows nothing of Ewan MacPhee. I tell you, day and night I suffer greater agony of spirit than any punishment the law could put upon me.

The Laird

PLEASE FEEL AT YOUR EASE, SIR. We stand on no ceremony here. The lodge may be rather grandly built but it is furnished, as you see, simply. Iron bedsteads and wicker chairs suffice in such wild natural surroundings. Nonetheless, I pride myself that my hospitality is not wanting. No one has ever risen from my table hungry. My guests, of whom I have many hundred in a season, are offered all that these rude mountains can provide in the way of game for the table and they seem well satisfied, for they almost always return to these parts. I will not offer you spirits, sir, as it is not the custom of the house during the day, but I have ordered that tea be brought.

I am informed that you come to seek information on Ewan MacPhee and, indeed, to pay him homage. I gather that on a journey from Glasgow to Inverness by the canal your steamer halted at Invergarry, where you were given an outline of MacPhee's colourful life. It strikes me as highly romantic that as a person bearing the same patronymic, you should wish to meet MacPhee to deliver a golden guinea into his hands as a token of your clan bond. But a caution at this juncture might not be misplaced. As a Glasgow man of commerce and a bailie, you live in as remote a condition of existence from MacPhee as it is conceivable to imagine. It is my opinion, sir, that my tenant will not receive you. Attempting to effect a meeting will be fraught with danger, especially if he thinks you to be part of a conspiracy against him.

The prospect from the window of this room is charming, is it not? On an autumn morning I believe it to be the best in the entire world, of which I have travelled much. The mountain opposite is called Gairich, which means the roaring of stags in the *Erse* language. Below it lies a shore fringed with arboreal vegetation and sand beaches. Do you see that small wooded island in the loch? The locals call it Eilean MhicPhee. That is where the man maintains his crude family habitation. Should you wish, sir, I will provide you with a boat and a ghillie to take you there to request audience at MacPhee's court – though I think effecting an interview with the Grand Vizier himself might be easier.

Once you have my account of the man's life and character, you may decide against attempting an interview, in which case rest assured that I will convey to MacPhee your best regards – and your guinea, which I venture he will accept. Whatever your decision, you are most welcome to rest the night here before proceeding on your way. When you next come this way your journey may be easier. I am presently engaged with certain other parties in raising the capital for a railway to Inverness. We are seeking parliamentary approval for this undertaking, which is sorely needed to open this wilderness and raise the standard of life endured by most of the population.

Possibly you know something of my family, sir? You will forgive me if I digress a little before discussing MacPhee himself, to explain how we came into possession of these wild parts. This estate came into our ownership only recently, in 1838, to be precise. A Puritan forebear of mine came to Scotland in the 1650s with Cromwell's army of occupation. On the restoration of the monarchy, he elected to stay in Scotland hoping to avoid the rampant restored Episcopacy south of the border. He settled in the north-east, in Aberdeenshire. A diligent man, he prospered there. Eventually my family became involved in the colonial trade, especially with Canada, where we maintained a large interest in the Hudson's Bay Company.

My own history is swiftly told. After education in Aberdeen, I spent time in Canada in wastes not unlike these around us – except that they are of far greater extent – and among aboriginals as exotic as MacPhee himself. Thereafter, I went into politics and became a member of Parliament for a Scottish constituency, a position I still hold. I have since attained cabinet office and count it as one of the achievements of my life to have steered Lord Grey's Reform Bill through the Commons in 1832. That bill established our constitution on as firm a foundation as is reasonably attainable. Some think it strange that, following that success, I refused a peerage. Perhaps I retain a residuum of my ancestor's republican sentiments. There have been social occasions here in this lodge where I have been the only man without a title. Being advanced in years, I do not relish further high office and, though I retain my Commons seat, I prefer to devote my energies to my business interests and to the improvement of conditions upon this estate, which were truly lamentable when I entered into occupancy.

Certain aspects of the history of this estate will enable you to appreciate the phenomenon of MacPhee, an active bandit in an epoch more civilised than any hitherto known.

Ah, tea is served. After you have refreshed yourself, I will resume my tale.

These lands were for generations owned by the most powerful of Highland clans, the MacDonnels of Glengarry. Their involvement in Jacobite Rebellions and an addiction to extravagance ultimately led to the bankruptcy of the Glengarry estate, allowing my purchase of various parts of the patrimony. The last Glengarry incumbent was a spendthrift who squandered his capital on lavish building projects and perverse entertainments in which animals were bizarrely killed. A tug of war using a live cow, until its limbs were torn from their sockets was his idea of amusement. His tenants were doubly burdened, with high rent and neglect. During the Napoleonic wars Glengarry raised a regiment of Fencibles, promising those who enlisted that they would be rewarded with land on their return from combat. That undertaking was conveniently forgotten and many of his tenants were shipped off to Canada.

When I came into possession of this estate more than half the population was destitute. I have been able to give them some seasonal work such as road building and tree planting, and have founded a school which offers a rudimentary education that is at least better than none at all. These efforts to ameliorate conditions have been rewarded – the population, so long in decline, has stabilised, and even increased a little lately.

But now to your fellow clansman, bailie. Of MacPhee's early life, I know little. Or rather, none of what I know is of undisputed veracity. MacPhee himself has told me of the wrongs he believes were done him in his youth, but others have given me accounts of the same events that are very much at variance with his own. The following would appear to bear some relationship with the truth. MacPhee, having fallen out with Glengarry, was pressed into military service during the wars with Bonaparte. He deserted, was captured, and then cheated the gallows by escaping a second time and making for the shores of Loch Arkaig where he lived for some time, later moving northwards. His present occupancy of his island kingdom began a short while before my acquisition of the estate.

His life in the years before we met is the stuff of legend, though he now portrays himself as a harmless grazier and claims he is persecuted simply because he will bend the knee to no man. The peasantry hold him in great regard and delight in embellishing his exploits. They see him as the one man who had the courage to stand against Glengarry. He is also cast as a necromancer possessed of magical powers. In the eyes of the local gentry, however, MacPhee is generally regarded as nothing more than a criminal – a poacher, a kidnapper and a murderer. For various reasons they fear to move against him.

In the context of such disparate points of view, I can vouch only for the veracity of what I have directly observed. I first set eyes on MacPhee about a decade ago, in this very room. Mr Mitchell, the railway engineer, was outlining the technical challenges involved in laying a railway track through the Grampian Mountains to Inverness, when a stranger entered the room. He cut an extremely dramatic figure, being well over six feet tall and dressed in full Highland garb – kilt, plaid, belted hose, and with a dirk at his side. Though not young, his features were handsome and well-chiselled. There was something absurdly theatrical about his evident self-regard, yet he was somehow impressive.

'To what do we owe the honour of your visit?' I enquired, attempting to conceal how startled I was.

'My name is Eoghann Ban Corie Bhuie.'

He paused. I waited till he spoke again, rather than repeat my question using a name I would surely mispronounce.

'You have taken these lands from Glengarry?'

I confirmed that I was, indeed, the new proprietor.

'I am your tenant,' he continued. 'My tack is the island they call Eilean MhicPhee.'

The title deeds to the lands I had purchased had said nothing about so colourful a tenant.

'By what right do you hold these lands, sir?' I asked.

In response, MacPhee strode towards us, drew his dirk and embedded it in the table where Mitchell and I sat.

'By this right I have it and by this right I will hold it!' he proclaimed.

'And what rent do you propose to pay for this property, sir?

Mitchell and I attempted to maintain an impassive demeanour as MacPhee again reached into the folds of his plaid. To our deep relief he produced an offering of peace, in the unlikely form of a large kebbuck of cheese, and promised me a yearly tribute of the same, if I left him to his business.

I raised an eyebrow at this excessively modest offer, wondering what his next gambit would be.

'In addition, I swear that while I live on the island no one shall touch your game, or do harm to you or what is yours.'

I had no doubt MacPhee could deliver such a promise, but the real reason I accepted was that the idea of having a bandit as my tenant thoroughly appealed – I fancied I would be the only proprietor in the kingdom able to claim this romantic distinction.

I proposed we shake hands on the deal, with Mitchell acting as witness.

'I need no papers or handshakes,' responded MacPhee, with a breathtaking arrogance. 'You have my word.' And with that, he turned on his heel and walked out.

Mitchell, who has a dry sense of humour, commented, 'You have won a fine dirk out of your transaction.'

'I have the bandit MacPhee,' I said. 'Why do you not keep the dirk yourself, as a memento of this incident.'

I did not see the outlaw again until the next appointed day – as deemed by MacPhee himself – when he turned up, again bearing a kebbuck of cheese, which I duly accepted as rent, for the estate had enjoyed a year free of poaching apart from the trifling depredations upon which MacPhee's family subsisted.

From these initial encounters, MacPhee took to visiting the Lodge more regularly, bringing offerings of game and specimens of illicit *aqua vitae* of his own manufacture. I confess that I rather enjoyed his company. Our conversations, normally took the form of a monologue on his part, prompted by occasional questions. He furnished me with much information about local customs and traditions. MacPhee was always willing to talk at length about his extraordinary adventures. For my part, it was a salutary experience to meet a man to whom my achievements in the spheres of commerce and politics were of absolutely no consequence. In his eyes I was of account only in respect of my ownership of the piece of barren and beautiful land where he lived out his days.

His tales concerning the injustices supposedly visited upon him by landlords, sheep-graziers and the military always showed him in a heroic light, overcoming all opponents by dint of insuperable physical strength and his peculiar brand of cunning. However, I observed that vigilant mistrust of his fellows had not altogether doused the fires of humanity in him and there was even a certain tenderness about him.

One foul November evening MacPhee arrived, bearing a pig of whisky, of which he, as usual, drank copiously while I, tasting it only in moderation and liberally laced with water, listened to his tales. A substantial fire of pine logs blazed in the hearth, something he regarded as an unnecessary and wasteful extravagance, even in the worst weather; doubtless the dubious heat of his own peat fire pleased him more. I was now comfortable enough with the bandit to jest, pointing to his whisky pig and the fire in turn, 'You have your indulgences, Mr MacPhee, and I have mine.'

The evening started as normal, with exchanges of pleasantries about the weather and the quality of the game that year, but before long MacPhee essayed upon familiar territory: he became extremely heated, saying that one of his daughters had been ill-treated by some shepherds working for a sheep grazier who had accused him of rustling stock and grazing goats without paying grass-mail.

With the intention of changing the drift of the conversation, I ventured to ask whether he had any sons. At this MacPhee fell silent, though I noticed the pig move a little as he grasped the handle in his mighty paw. I gave him time to compose himself. This he soon did, continuing in a voice devoid of its former ferocity, 'I had two sons. Both are dead.'

I commiserated, leaving it to him as to whether he wished to unburden himself further.

'There is a deep pool,' he said, 'where the river runs out of the loch and winds through a narrow channel of rock. This is known to be the home of a *tarbh-uisge*. My children were warned never to go near the pool but my son and one of his sisters went there to play. The girl told us that the *tarbh-uisge* came out of the water and offered the boy a ride on its back. Though she warned him not to, he mounted the beast. But his hands instantly stuck to its back and when it dived, the *tarbh-uisge* took the boy with him. We found his body downstream, with all the skin torn from his poor hands. He is buried on my island. I made his coffin myself, out of herring boxes left from the previous winter.'

It was not the moment to point out that there were perfectly natural explanations for the drowning and the scarred palms of the corpse. Instead, I gently enquired, 'But you mentioned two sons?'

Clearly in the grip of overwhelming emotion, MacPhee rose to his feet. All he said before leaving was, 'That is a story I can never tell.' It is one I have yet to hear.

I feared that I had risked our friendship in encouraging this exposure of his vulnerability, but fortunately my neighbour did not cease his visits. He grew willing to mingle with my guests, to whom he was an object of astonishment and wonder. MacPhee treated them with a slight condescension that betrayed his lack of regard for the aristocracy. He delighted in recounting his adventures and was evidently gratified whenever he was asked to pose for a portrait by the ladies, or some visiting artist. He was always paid for these sittings and those who were over-generous I would playfully chide with corrupting my bandit.

MacPhee is now an old man. His serious felonies lie in the past, at a distance of a quarter century. His present misdemeanours are of a minor and colourful nature. Though he is still technically under edict of outlawry, I believe the authorities are disposed to let him extinguish his life naturally here in the wilderness. However, he has lately acquired a powerful and deadly enemy in Mr Cameron of Corriechoille, a rich sheep grazier who utilises extensive territories for his undertaking. He retains grazing rights on my lands under a long lease given by Glengarry, which I am obliged to observe. That MacPhee takes a few of his sheep and abuses his grazings is in little doubt, though this can surely be of trifling economic import to Cameron, who drives 100,000 beasts to Falkirk tryst every year.

I confess that I find Cameron to be a singularly unpleasant man, ugly, dirty and with a dribbling mouth, which he constantly wipes with his sleeve. It is said that he so parsimonious that he subsists on bread and cheese alone. Certainly, his wealth has endowed him with nothing of civility or humanity. The peasantry hold him in real terror – he has often enforced evictions to defend his grazing leases. MacPhee's attitude infuriates him and he fears the bandit's example is influencing others. On this subject he recently requested an audience with me. I gained the impression that Cameron contemplates the manufacture of some incident to rekindle MacPhee's notoriety and force the authorities to take action against him. I offered to buy out his grazing rights but he refused, with much insincere grovelling which failed to conceal his contempt for my concern with the bandit's welfare.

What the future holds for MacPhee I know not. I have reason to fear for the man and shall do everything I can to protect him.

Now, would you enjoy a walk in the grounds before dinner? I am intrigued to hear whether you still intend to contact your namesake.

The Grazier

MY NAME IS JOHN CAMERON, called Corriechoille after the place of my origins. My grandfather came to that place, in the time of the Forfeit Commissioners, to take over the lease of a man who had been killed in the Rebellion. My grandfather became the tacksman, collecting the rents for the Commissioners, which none else would do, they all being Locheil's men.

When Locheil returned he took my own father on as tacksman. While many of the tenants were away in the wars against the monzies, my father sub-let their lands and turned them over to black cattle which were then fetching premium prices. He made good money droving them to Crieff or Falkirk, where they were salted and barrelled for the Army. But he was a man who took nothing for granted. He foresaw that after the war, cattle prices would not hold. Also, he observed that some landowners in the Highlands were already looking to sheep for their prosperity. When I was a boy he advised me the future was in sheep. That advice has stood me in good stead.

The Commissioners were fair with the tenantry, though they got but little thanks. The rents they gathered were returned to the community in the form of roads, harbours and kirks. But for all that the Commissioners encouraged them to move with the times, the tenants waited in dumb loyalty for the return of their chiefs, who, when they did eventually return, were no wiser than before and, if it were possible, even greedier for siller. The first thing they did was to rack up the rents, but they did nothing to improve the land. Any fool could see that with the end of the war, the tenants' profits from cattle would drop and they would be unable to pay the rents. And that's exactly what did happen. But the demand for wool held up. The landlords saw that sheep need but little looking after. The logic of the situation was inescapable: the glens must be cleared to make way for the sheep. The tenants had blinded themselves with sentiment in staying loyal to their chiefs. They followed them in the disastrous Jacobitical cause, then the same men led them off to war on the Hanoverian cause. Now their reward was to be eviction. Yet the one they curse for their misfortunes is myself, who in no way caused their situation, though I will not deny that I have managed to turn circumstances to my advantage and profit.

As a boy, I spent much time with my father on his business. Though I have nothing against learning, I never attended school. For many, it simply makes of them fools who can read and write. I needed only the education of watching my father and learning from him; what I cannot do, I now have the means to hire lawyers and suchlike to do for me. Much the best learning was walking with a stick in my hand, barefoot, from Lochaber to the tryst, following the old routes through the mountains – the cattle did not like the hard military roads. I was shown how to drive the beasts with dogs and where to find the places of water and grass. Once there was a blindrift on the pass and the animals were smoored. My father dug a hole beside the belly of a stickit cow and I spent the night against its udders with the dogs, while he sought the beasts' safety. He would not abandon an animal. In the morning he slashed the cow with his dirk and made me eat the warm blood mixed with oats and snow, till we found food and warmth at the Spittal. This knowledge is not to be found in books.

People forget that my father quit employment as the tacksman when Locheil told him to clear the people. They forget that he said to Locheil's face, 'I will collect your rents, but I will not evict a man from his living.' He lost his position, and when he had to sell his cattle cheap after Waterloo he lost money, though far less than many others, so that when he died I was not forced to shift or become a day-labourer. People speak against him as they speak against myself, forgetting his sacrifice.

As I have said, my father foresaw the coming of the sheep. He started grazing on his own account in a small way, subletting land from local cottars. Soon however, new men came in, men with names like Sword, Lockhart and Hogg. They brought with them the blackface from the Borders and took up residence at the abandoned clachans on Locheilside and in Glengarry. These new residents did not know the country or its language, but they knew their job well enough in terms of clipping and shearing. The lairds, however, knew as little of sheep as they knew of anything, and could not manage the business properly. They had no interest except in the money, and that way a man will never prosper.

I started business in a small way, leasing a modest portion of ground and putting my own sheep and my own men on it. I knew the routes and the ways of the market, and took on more land. The lairds got their yearly rent, they cared little about anything else. Eventually, most of them gave up altogether at playing grazier and leased all of their grazing rights to me. Though I did not own even the ground my house stood on, I had twenty thousand sheep, a hundred men in my employ and the title to graze almost every blade of grass between the Great Glen and the western sea.

I worked hard for my winnings. I worked my men hard as well, though I flatter myself they were loyal; no man ever left my employment, but that I dismissed him for dishonesty or idleness. The people's hearts were set hard against me so I was careful always to have some of my men with me, ready to repel assault. As it was, I was subject only to verbal abuse. Much as I wished to be impervious, these insults hurt me as much as a blow. These peasants fawned on Glengarry, who wasted his patrimony on cruel games with dumb beasts. They scraped before Locheil, who built for himself a house that would have sheltered hundreds, while they lived in hovels of clod and undressed stone. Yet I was hated. I, whose work brought so much money into Lochaber.

For thirty years I never missed a tryst at Falkirk or Crieff. I rode in wind, hail and snow over roads and passes, my only sustenance a crust of bread. I dressed in the same clothes as my men, and slept on the ground with them around the fire at night. The one luxury I allowed myself was to cover the roof of my house with Ballachulish slate and put glass in the windows, otherwise it was a house as any other. My men often suffered abuse when they took their ease at an inn. Worse, dykes which required much labour to build were knocked down, letting the sheep stray. Whatever any man say against me, I would grudge no starving pauper a sheep that might not be his own. But it is a matter altogether different when I find dozens of my beasts with their throats cut, left dying on the moor. These irritations and offences I could not tolerate.

When MacPhee arrived back from the wars, everyone in Lochaber had heard of his enforced enlistment and his desertion. I was even inclined to sympathise with the man. He showed more spirit than the rest of the broken people in these parts. I had no dispute with him.

However, as fresh tales of his exploits rolled in, it became clear there was a vicious side to MacPhee. He was far from being the victim of circumstances he wanted people to believe he was. Violent assaults and at least one murder were attributed to his hand. Then came the news that he had abducted and ravished a young girl from Knoydart and was holding her against her will. Later, for her shame, the girl had to claim that she had gone with him willingly.

MacPhee made his living by various means. He certainly roamed the hills poaching deer and salmon. Other poachers had been sent to Van Diemen's Land and his audacious evasion of arrest enhanced his status in the eyes of the peasantry. He reputedly made illicit *usquebaugh* in a modest way and prepared medicines from herbage such as the *lus an laoigh* to cure cattle. The superstitious peasantry believed him able to cast spells to secure the return of amorous affections, or other particular ends. These practises were of little harm, and none to myself. Had he continued only in them, MacPhee would doubtless have been forgotten by the law, especially as his serious crimes distanced themselves in the past.

Possibly he may have started to believe his own tales of his invincibility. At any rate, MacPhee began to cross me in a most provocative way that finally forced me to respond – much against my will, for I knew any retaliation would only increase the malevolence of the peasantry towards myself.

MacPhee had a herd of goats which his children would tend while he was off on his business. Doubtless the rigours of the chase were becoming harder for him at his age. It had become the rule for landowners of sporting estates to protect their profits by employing ghillies. Taking a deer was not as easy as it once was.

While in itself, the little grass MacPhee's goats ate I did not grudge, despite what they say, the problem was that, what he did, others imitated. On numerous occasions, my men found cattle or sheep belonging to local people grazing in the richer pastures of the glens, which I pay good money to have for my exclusive use. When challenged, the miscreants would reply that MacPhee grazed his goats on my land, so why could they not do likewise? This was a precedent I could not allow to be established.

A suitable opportunity to challenge MacPhee arose at a market in the Garrison. As usual, I was attended by half a dozen of my men. We were there to purchase necessaries for a drove which was about to take place, see to the shoeing of the garrons, procure supplies and so forth. Despite the benefits my custom brings to the traders, their business with me is always done with some comment of ill-will and it is seldom I can avoid paying above normal rates for my goods. They always say that I can well afford it.

I was taking refreshment at a hawker's booth, when someone mentioned that MacPhee was at the market, disposing of some of his kebbucks and a couple of older goats. I realised that if I failed to confront him now, everyone would think I feared the outlaw. I resolved to seek a resolution of the issue.

I went over to the stall where he squatted with his wares and picked up one of his cheeses, holding out a coin in payment, and as evidence of my good will. He made a play of pretending not to see me and continued his discussion with another customer. This angered me into saying what I had not intended.

'Mr MacPhee, I hear you graze your goats on my land, without paying me grass-mail.'

He pointedly carried on conversing for a few minutes as though he had not heard me and then stood slowly, with ridiculous assumed dignity.

'The land belongs to the *Sassunach* Ellice. The grass belongs to

God. I owe you nothing, Cameron.'

I continued, attempting reason.

'I have the legal rights to the grazing, MacPhee, rights I have paid for. I do not grudge you a morsel of grass for your goats and wish your family no ill, but you must give some token of my rights, as an example to others. Deliver me two goats a year and we will say no more on the matter.'

'Damn the goat of mine you lay hands on, Corriechoille,' he flamed and leapt forward, as if to attack me. It took all of my men to hold him and I was unable to prevent one of them striking him a severe blow. The cry went up and we were surrounded by a rabble armed with dirks and clubs. MacPhee was clearly gratified at the sight.

'Tell your men to leave me be, Cameron,' he scoffed, 'or there will be serious work done here.'

I ordered him to be freed. My men immediately took up position around me. MacPhee refrained from whipping up the crowd's anger against us, content with his perceived victory. As he dismissed us from his stall, his kebbuck was crushed against my coat and he laughed that I could keep it as my rent. Then he indicated that I should reclaim my coin, which lay in the dirt.

'Keep it for your wares,' I said as a parting shot, 'lest you claim you are not now in my debt, for so you remain.'

There is an imputation against me that I plot MacPhee's downfall. Nothing could be further from the truth. I have stayed my hand till provoked beyond endurance. I was disposed to let the issue rest, despite MacPhee's refusal to pay a token grass-mail, but matters worsened. Reports of broken dykes and slaughtered sheep accumulated. MacPhee himself may not have been the author of all these acts, some were doubtless committed by others following his example, knowing that suspicion would rest upon the outlaw. MacPhee began to extend his depredations: sheep disappeared off the hill. It was impossible to watch over every one. He had turned sheep rustler. I had no direct proof, though the word was that he started to deal in tallow and sheepskins. At the Garrison he would boast of his exploits, saying that Cameron was nothing but a scared sheep himself.

Such insults do not trouble me. Sheep stealing does. The stock on the hills was protected only by the respect for the law; if that went, I would have to hire every shepherd in Scotland to protect my flocks. But I had no proof the sheep MacPhee were selling were mine, so I had to bide my time. One day, it was reported that there had been sightings of sheep among his goats at Loch Quoich, so I instructed my men to go and ascertain by the ear markings whether any of my sheep were there and if so, to drive them off as evidence. Knowing MacPhee was absent, I sent the men unarmed.

They surprised MacPhee's children at their herding and discovered several of my sheep amongst the goats. My men attempted to drive them away with their dogs, at which the bandit's brood attacked them with stones and fistfuls of animal manure. At that point there came firing from the island, causing dogs, goats and sheep to scatter in terror. MacPhee's wife was the one firing at my men. They retreated out of range and were forced to return without the sheep, but with the certainty that MacPhee was living off my labours. I had no option but to restrain him, or see my work destroyed.

The question was how best to effect my resolve. To obtain evidence of his rustling and undertake legal action would be a long process. I conceived it would be a speedier remedy to obtain an order against his property for non-payment of grazing costs. As I expected, he failed to attend the hearing and his goats were awarded to me, as payment, by the court. MacPhee was properly informed by letter, but failed to respond. The postman had to be provided with an armed military guard to be persuaded to deliver that letter, which shows the reputation MacPhee now enjoyed.

The news of the legal ruling reached Ellice, who took over part of Glengarry's lands for his sporting pleasures some time ago. His type is even worse than the old chiefs. They live on their wealth, do nothing, and use the land for worthless sport, land which could be used for grazing. He asked me to come and see him at an appointed time, as if I was his servant. I am not a wilful man and though he thought, and said, that I had thereby slighted him, I had business and could not attend his summons till later.

He was most discourteous, inviting me neither to sit nor sup after my twenty-mile journey to see him, asking instead to buy out my grazing rights. He accused me of meditating ill towards MacPhee, whom he portrayed as a harmless, even heroic, figure. His offer was worth double the grazings, but had it been a hundredfold I would not have accepted. That would have been tantamount to surrender and that I could not do without harming my reputation and business. Ellice disregarded my reasonable suggestion that he use his authority to tell MacPhee to acknowledge my rights and give up his rustling. Ellice implied that I was motivated in the matter by greed. We parted on ill terms.

On returning home, I summoned my head shepherd and instructed him to have MacPhee's den watched and, next time he was away, to collect our goats, as was our legal right. I gave him full discretion on how it might be done, but to be sure to do it, and bring the goats to our fanks at Invergarry.

My intention was only to use the goats as a bargaining counter:

if MacPhee stopped his raiding and acknowledged my superiority on the land, he would have them back.

My men went one night to MacPhee's stockade opposite Eilean MhicPhee. The children watching over them had to be restrained, though my men deny inflicting any hurt upon them. Despite cover of darkness, MacPhee's woman detected their presence and again she fired at them. One man sustained a shoulder injury from a shot.

I could not have anticipated the ensuing escalation of events. I did not realise the depths of infamy to which MacPhee, in his outraged vanity, would descend. He descended with his fiend of a wife and beat the man watching the goats near to death then tied him fast and threw him into the loch, where he all but drowned. That his mad witch of a wife would set fire to the inn where my men were relaxing with others who were in no way involved in our dispute, is barely credible. She shot at those issuing from the building. One man was crushed to death in the panic and another horribly burned to death.

Their culpability for these heinous deeds is naturally contested by the pair, but there are numerous witnesses, of greater credibility than they.

It is imperative that MacPhee be punished for these crimes. He deserves to hang. However, his wife may be viewed in some respects as being herself his victim and, considering also the plight of her children, some way might be found to mitigate the severity of the law in her case.

The Wife

THE PANEL, HELEN MACPHEE, BORN Macpherson, has had the following statement read back to her in Gaelic by the minister, Reverend Fraser, who previously heard her original deposition in that tongue, and rendered it into English. The panel asserts that what follows is a true account of the events of her life, with particular regard to that period spent with Ewan MacPhee, outlaw, whom she designates as her husband. She attests this with her thumb mark, witnessed by the Reverend Fraser.

John Blackie, Procurator-Fiscal
Fort William. 21 April, 1850

This I assert, on pain of eternal damnation and the rigours of the law in relation to perjury, to be a true account of events which preceded my coming here with my family to the Garrison and to prison.

Helen MacPhee

What is your name, parentage and place of birth?
My name is Helen MacPhee, formerly Macpherson. I was born in the Rough Bounds at a place called Barrisdale, in the Year of Waterloo, the year the men came home from the wars with money in their pockets. Many were the joyful women in Barrisdale but my mother was not amongst them, for when she had heard that

her husband Hector Macpherson was slain, she had taken another man, who deserted her when she fell pregnant. Her relief that Hector was still alive was tempered by fear at his reaction to the sight of a child he had not fathered. My mother told me that for a week he said nothing of it. He must have been thinking what to do. Then he ordered her to leave, with the words, 'Go to the man whose child this is.'

People spoke against him but no one would challenge him on my mother's behalf. She moved into a byre belonging to some neighbours, the Campbells, and depended on their charity until I was old enough for her to take work. She was too poorly to work in the fields or at the herring but she managed to secure a position as a servant at the big house of Barrisdale. She died, worn out with grief, when I was ten years old.

Hector had put his money from the army into cattle and became a drover, taking a few beasts over the mountains to Crieff every year. Thus he was able to pay his rent without working his land, which he leased to others. Being better off than most in the clachan gave him a high opinion of himself, but he hid his loneliness in drinking, and his filthy house was a scandal. Everyone said that before the wars Hector was kind but that he had changed since his return.

Times were hard for everyone. There was no more money from soldiering and the herring shoals were fickle. Rent could not be paid in the bad years. The people could hardly feed their own families, let alone me. They told Hector that since he needed someone to look after his house and I needed a roof over my head, he should take me in.

And so as a servant I went to his house. He was not cruel to me, he did not hit me – though when he was drunk he railed against my mother. He worked me hard, for all that he was a slovenly man. I cherished the thought of leaving. Each season I kept the pay he gave me, saving against the day I could depart. When he was away I took extra work as a gleaner at harvest time or packing herring at Kinlochhourn. I had to pledge everyone to secrecy, for Hector had forbidden me to work as a day-labourer.

How came you first to know Ewan MacPhee, the outlaw?
My life continued in this wretched way until the day MacPhee crossed the threshold. He was about Hector's age, yet he had none of the mean-spirited bitterness that tainted Hector's features. I immediately knew that here was a man I would follow anywhere. He was fine looking, tall and bold. When I told him Hector was away droving he said, 'Let him know Eoghann Ban Corrie Bhuie will be back.' And then he added, 'How is it that such a fine woman as yourself comes to have no husband?'

A month later he returned. He and Hector sat drinking whisky by the fire, talking over some business matter. I removed myself to the corner of the room, carrying on with my wool carding. They spoke in whispers but as the drink flowed they spoke more openly, forgetting me. Ewan was trying to sell cattle to Hector, who was offering him a derisory price. I heard the words, 'The only other offer you will get from me, MacPhee, will be a halter.'

Nonetheless they remained cordial and after they struck their deal they carried on in fine fettle. My father was in better spirits than I could recall, and he even brought out his pipes to play to his guest. When I served their food, Ewan smiled in thanks.

All was harmony until after the meal, when something was said that almost made me drop my carding comb.

'Hector, I would have that fine lass of yours as my wife. What do you say?'

My father flew into a temper. 'You are forgetting you are an outlaw and a thief. How dare you think to marry the daughter of an independent man? Leave my house.'

MacPhee rose slowly and I thought it likely he would assault the man who now claimed to be my father. But he spoke in a measured way, at which I was greatly impressed. 'You have no objection to doing business with me, or drinking my whisky,' he said. 'But you object when I offer to give this child a better life. Your treatment of her is an abomination throughout the lands of Glengarry. I shall cause no affray here in your house where we have broken bread together, but be assured I will repay you for this, Macpherson.'

MacPhee left with the dignity of a prince and then my father railed against me, saying that I was a harlot like my mother. He struck me for the first and only time. I thought to have seen the last of the man I had hoped might free me. Hector treated me with ever greater contempt, whether drunk or sober. He was away less often, as the cattle trade was in difficulties, and he was forced to soil his hands with making lazy-beds and collecting seaweed for manure. This put him, despite his affectations, at no remove from the other cottars. Daily his moods grew worse.

How shifted you to Glenquoich with MacPhee and was that done willingly on your part?
Hector was away and I was preparing to retire at an early hour, for the next day I faced the eight-mile walk to Kinlochhourn, where I was to labour during his absence. Without even a knock, the door opened and in came MacPhee.

All he said was, 'Take only what is yours, and come. We will be man and wife my lass, if you will.'

He unwrapped his great plaid, put it around me and threw me over his back like a sack of peats. I only had time to tell him where my meagre hoard of coins lay, before he carried me out into the night, never more to see Barrisdale.

The journey was no more a discomfort than if I had been conveyed on the back of a fine stallion. After several hours and many miles, as dawn was breaking in the east, he transported me in his boat across the dark loch to an island where he had built a cabin with his own hands, away from the eyes of men. There he stayed unmolested, protected by the power of his reputation. I was married there as a Christian, as the minister standing in this room can testify, for he himself carried out the ceremony and can assent to my willingness. Hector has made false accusations at law against my husband, saying he abducted me and used me for his lust and that I was not of an age to marry.

I know from Ewan's telling that all the charges that had been raised against him over the years were untrue, or concerned actions he had been forced to commit in self-defence. Nonetheless, it was certain that if we moved to a less secluded spot he would be arrested and then none of the mighty would believe him.

How did MacPhee make his living?
Ewan was a good provider, always a considerate and affectionate husband. I bore him five children, though only the boy, who later drowned, and the two girls survived infancy. Ewan was often away hunting or fishing in the mountains. Occasionally he travelled far afield to earn money to procure oats, which would not grow in the cold and wet of Glenquoich. Our main livelihood was the herd of goats which we had originally paid for with my *tocher*. They gave

us meat, milk and wool. The children tended them, and I made the cheese and carded their wool, which Ewan sold. It is a dreadful lie to say that we lived by stealing. We worked hard and troubled no one, as long as they left us untroubled.

It is true we paid no rent to Glengarry, but no one ever came to demand any. When Mr Ellice arrived in the glen Ewan went to the big house and made a bargain with him. Apart from the minister and the gentlemen who came to teach the children their catechism no one ever came to the island. I believe we would have lived out our days there in peace, but for Corriechoille, that man of wickedness.

Give your account of your dispute with Cameron, the grazier you call Corriechoille.

We graze our goats on the ancestral lands of MacDonnel, as our forefathers have done since time immemorial. Mr Ellice made it clear that he had no objection to our residence and grazing on his lands. And then one day comes a man from Corriechoille, shouting on the shore that he wishes to speak with MacPhee. No man had ever had such temerity before. I told him Ewan was away, but he said he would wait. After some hours my husband came down off the slopes of Gairich. I did not hear their conversation clearly, but Ewan told me that the man came with the message that Corriechoille had a lease on the grass on these hillsides and that if we grazed our goats we must pay grass-mail, otherwise Corriechoille would remove the beasts. It came to shouting. Corriechoille's man attacked my husband. Though Ewan is always armed, he resisted the temptation of dirk or gun against an unarmed man and engaged in combat by fisticuffs. He gave the fellow a good hiding and sent him off with his tail between his legs and a message that if Corriechoille wanted the goats removed, he should come and see to it himself.

'How can one man own the land, and another claim to own the grass that grows upon it?' Ewan asked me. I urged him to go to Mr Ellice and ask for his aid. But he said he could manage such a poor thing as Corriechoille without troubling the new laird.

Corriechoille is the richest man in all Lochaber, richer than Locheil, richer even than Mr Ellice. His fortune has been made from making paupers of the people. In Glenquoich, in the years before I came to live here, he hounded folk from their houses, or burned them about their ears to make them shift. Any caught giving shelter to those who had been evicted were evicted themselves. People were so desperate they lived in caves or in the woods. It was a terrible time. Women gave birth to dead children and men went mad. This Corriechoille, who has grown rich on misery, cannot abide to see Ewan cross his commands. He wishes to destroy my husband.

Narrate more particularly some incidents of the dispute.
The next incident came one day when I was sitting outside in the fine weather at my carding when I heard a commotion over on the shore where the girls were tending the goats. I saw some of Corriechoille's men striking the children and attempting to drive the goats away. Ewan was away in the mountains and had left his boat at the other side of the lochside. I realised I was unable to cross the water to protect my girls. I ran to the house and took up two of my husband's rifles, which he kept loaded. Corriechiolle's men say I fired at them. They are liars and cowards, who ran from a woman. Would I fire at them when they were so near my own children? I fired into the air, only that, to affright them and hoping to attract Ewan. Corriechiolle's men ran like sheep. The girls chased

after them, pelting them with stones.

Afterwards two score of Corriechiolle's sheep were found with their throats cut. Ewan was blamed. But he would have had no part in such wanton slaughter – he would have seen it as a waste of good meat and wool. Someone with a grudge against Corriechoille used Ewan's reputation as a shield.

From then on we kept a close watch on our goats, knowing Corriechoille would return to seek his revenge. Why is that wicked man not lying on a cold floor, charged with his crimes instead of ourselves, the innocent victims of his rage? Ask the people of Glengarry and Knoydart who is the criminal! Is it Ewan, who took nothing from them, who doctored their cattle for a trifle and who, in the time of famine, came to those who had helped him, to clachans all the way from Barrisdale to the Dark Mile, to give them a fish or a beast he had taken? Or is it Corriechoille, who has driven men from the lands which their families had worked for generations?

The next thing, a letter came, brought by a man in a uniform who gave it to one of the girls at the lochside and instructed her to pass it to their father. She read what she could of its words, which were hard to understand. One thing we could understand was that Coirriechoille had an order from the authorities to possess our goats, because they claimed we were due him grass-mail.

'He cannot own our goats,' Ewan said, 'any more than he owns the grass.' For many nights my husband slept with the goats in their stockade.

When Corriechoille struck again, it was once more the deed of a man suckled on coward's milk. Ewan was at the Garrison and must have been espied there, or they would not have dared to come. And even then, they came in the night. They bound and sorely beat my daughter who was with the goats. I heard their dogs barking and the goats bleating as they tried to drive them away. The blaze of their torches lit up the shoreline. When I took up the gun this time I did not aim to miss. I fired below the torches and heard more than one scream before their lights disappeared down the glen. That night I wept sorely, fearing that even my Ewan could not overcome this latest affront.

And so your husband and yourself plotted a dreadful revenge?
Ewan intended only to repossess what was ours and to frighten off Corriechoille's men. When he came back a few days after the goats had been taken, he had already heard the news. Corriechoille and his men were boasting of their blow against Ewan, who you might remember was now a man of more than sixty summers. For some time he pondered, weary and depressed, and I felt that he might be inclined to accept this latest injustice inflicted upon him. Corriechoille, he told me, had taken our goats to Invergarry where they were held in a stockade, to be sold at the next mart. On the second day Ewan told me to pack supplies for the journey. We travelled at night, on foot, until we reached the clachan of Tomdoun, where we obtained garrons from a friend. We came to Invergarry in the middle of the second night. Ewan left me with the garrons while he went through the woods to where the goats were kept. He soon returned to tell me they were well guarded by several men, but that he had a plan. I speak the truth when I say we intended no harm.

We tethered the garrons and Ewan went back to the stockade to wait. I approached the inn nearby, where sound of revelry indicated that the rest of Corriechoille's men were celebrating their victory. There was a byre next to the inn, containing little but rubbish. Striking a couple of stones to a handful of straw it was a moment's work to start a fire, which Ewan reasoned would draw the watchers away from his goats. There was no intention to harm anyone. Had there been, I would have fired the inn itself.

The blazing byre soon brightened the night and, as expected, the goat watchers ran to raise the alarm with their companions at the inn, leaving only one guard. He was easily overpowered. We released our beasts quickly, indeed, Ewan could herd them as if by magic, with his whistles and cries. Very soon we were on our return journey to Loch Quoich. The blaze behind us was not abating, the flames reddened the skies. We had other things on our minds. Later we found out that the drunken graziers in the inn thought their companions were jesting and refused to believe there was a fire until it was too late.

A man was crushed to death and another fatally burned. Several witnesses say that you set the hostelry ablaze, not the byre, and that you fired shots into the building.

They lie, or they err due to their drunkenness. I regret the deaths, but we in no way intended them.

All the way back to Glenquoich, Ewan was silent, as if defeated. I had expected him to be triumphant. We returned the goats to their stockade. The goats were depleted from their original numbers taken by Corriechoille. Only on crossing to the island did my husband break his silence, saying, 'They will not leave us alone this time, Helen.'

He spoke truly.

Ewan cleaned and loaded his rifles, and paced around looking out for attackers. They came two days later. The coward Corriechoille had sent for the soldiery. Of course, he himself was not there, though some of his men were. We could see about twenty soldiers taking up positions on the shore, as if to subject us to siege. We covered the children with sheepskins, the only protection we had for them. I took up a rifle and went to where Ewan stood at a large rock, parleying with the men on the shore. In response to a demand to give himself up, he stepped from behind the rock and fired, roaring, 'That is my answer!'

I added the sound of my rifle to his.

The response was like the roaring of the thunder on the mountains. For many moments it was so intense we could only shelter behind our rock while branches scattered by the bullets fell around us. After this fusillade another demand to surrender was made. The house behind us had been hit, our children inside were screaming. Ewan instructed me to take the rifles back to the cabin and attend to the girls. He stepped from behind the rock and shouted in a clear strong voice that he was surrendering. He took his boat from its place of concealment and began to row across to the mainland, under the muzzles of many rifles. I thought they would kill him as he rowed, but he gained the shore. There the soldiers put irons on him. I saw with my own eyes some of Corriechoille's men lunge at him and strike him.

Two days later, after selling the goats and the possessions we could not carry with us, I walked here to my husband in prison, bringing our children and what little money I have. What justice is this for us to be charged as murderers at the wishes of a man such as Corriechoille.

I cannot read or write, but I do know this: what they call justice is nothing more than a plaything of the rich and mighty. There is no justice for the poor. I am where I should be, with my husband and children. We shall live or die together. Do your worst, sir, as you will.

The Minister

THE TEXT FOR MY SERMON TODAY IS 'Render unto Caesar that which is Caesar's'.

As you all should know, obedience to the authorities constituted under God is the basis of civil society. Those who presume to pull down legitimate government are causing discord and chaos. Need we look further than the distemper which has seized our workmen in the manufacturing districts? Though they may indeed suffer wrongs, they are misled under the banner of Chartism, to put government in the hands of the vulgar and communalise property. Do we not see a similar folly in the self-styled 'Free' Kirk, which seeks to terminate the influence of patrons, lay and landed, in Kirk affairs, and to place the government of the most noble reformed Kirk in Christendom under the direction of unfettered democracy? In such troubled times, those charged with the spiritual welfare of the populace, must do everything in their power to emphasise the necessity of obedience to the law. Regard the Republican convulsions that overtook France and be grateful that we live under the protection of constitutional government.

It saddens me to have to say that even here in this remote parish, we have not been spared the spirit of faction and schism. Upwards of one-third of this congregation, whose spiritual needs I have ministered to during a full thirty years, have taken up with the seceders. They are an affront to good religion. Maintaining my manse and stipend has become fraught with difficulty for the Established Kirk because of their wrong-headed actions. However, the Lord has sent me travails before, and I do not flinch at the prospect of material hardship. When I arrived in this parish, chosen as you know by the patron, I realised that some hearts were against me. I laboured long in the vineyard to win over the hostile and the doubting, labours which I thought had been crowned with success. Yet I see many of those who spoke against me are now in league with the seceders. Be assured, their subversive efforts will fail. Not only is the hand of civil power against them, but also against them is the hand of the Lord.

So far, every landlord within a distance of twenty miles has refused to lease land to them on which to build a kirk. Consequently, they have constructed a replica of the Ark and moored in the loch as their place worship. The good Lord will punish them with winter gales and storms and they will tire of the meagre spiritual fare offered them in sermons that denounce the patrons and demand democratic principles in church government. Their preachers vilify landlords and graziers and inflame the tenantry to resist agricultural improvements and schemes of emigration. Moreover, it seems that the new landlord in Glenquoich has added his voice to that of the sectaries, printing pamphlets about supposed injustice to the tenantry and even raising these specious points in parliament. Perhaps we should have expected little better from Mr Ellice, whose ancestors were strangers to this land and who came to Scotland with the republican and sectary Cromwell.

The Lord is not to be mocked. To chastise us, He has sent poor harvests and the blight of the potato crop. Many tenants are in such a miserable state that they cannot pay their rents. It must be seen that their landlords have no alternative but to procure the removal of the indigent to the colonies. In this work the charitable assistance has been forthcoming from those who understand that it is in the best interests of all. They err, even though they be well-meaning, who attempt to impede this necessary unburdening of the land from its surplus population. The road to Hell is paved with good intentions.

These introductory remarks bring me to the difficult matter of which I wish to speak today. I know that the congregation sitting before me this Sabbath consists of those sound in both religious and civil matters. But the spirit of faction and rebellion extends far and wide, and often we are most blind to our lapses of duty closest to home.

There lies in jail near this holy Kirk a man called Ewan MacPhee who is accused of murder, treason and kidnapping. The civil authorities have been presented with all manner of excuses and evasions by those asked to perform jury service in this case and I must ask all of you gathered here on this Sabbath day to look into your hearts and if any of you are so summoned, find written therein a clear understanding of your responsibility to the civil authorities.

I myself was recently called upon to report to the Kirk Session the history of my relations with Ewan MacPhee. In order that the record might be set straight I have been given leave by the elders to read out my deposition to the session.

WHEN I FIRST CAME INTO this parish as a young minister, I was astonished to discover that my charge of souls included a bandit. The extirpation of the Jacobite distemper many decades before and the introduction of law, good government and sound religious principles had, I thought, eliminated all such. But in this modern age, there still lurked in the wilds this outlaw who faced execution if apprehended.

From my parishioners I learned the power he exerted over the local population. By usage of charms, herbs and other nonsense, he is reputed to be some sort of a doctor, especially of animals. The superstitious also believe he can cast spells cursing those who harm him. I heard that he had prodigious strength and was always equipped with instruments of execution, which practice is in direct contravention of the law. An innocent chapman was stabbed, narrowly escaping with his life, for simply asking MacPhee directions on the road. To MacPhee's suspicious mind, any stranger asking questions had to be an agent of his arrest. The assault was meant as a warning to others who might think of betraying him. MacPhee's supporters thought nothing of misdirecting the civil authorities in their pursuit and he found free quarter all the way from the Great Glen to the Rough Bounds, where the misguided populace revere him as a hero waging war for the poor against the landlords and graziers. The man may indeed possess some redeeming qualities, but it is certain that in him these qualities are wasted. Talents bestowed by our Lord are intended to be applied only through law-abiding routes.

A few years after taking up my charge in the parish, I had my first opportunity to ascertain the man's qualities first hand. MacPhee had gone to ground and little had been heard of him for some time; it was said that he had moved from Loch Arkaigside further into the wilds, nearer to Loch Quoich. I was at supper in the manse, attended only by my housekeeper, an excellent local woman, though somewhat prone to superstition. It was not a pleasant night and I settled myself by the fireside, intending to seek inspiration from the Bible. There was a sudden altercation at the rear of the house and my housekeeper rushed into the room saying, 'There is someone here wanting to see you. It is MacPhee himself.' Behind her stood an imposing figure, drenched to the skin, clutching in both hands the bonnet he had taken off in respect of my office.

Knowing the man's reputation, I admit to feeling acute anxiety at finding myself in his presence. I meditated that his purpose was to plunder the house. To my astonishment he announced in an imperious tone, that I should get my Bible and go with him. 'You are to marry me,' he said. 'My bride waits at Loch Quoich.'

I ventured that the marriage ceremony should be performed on a more suitable occasion, and properly arranged with the session clerk. I added that I would be delighted to see him at the Kirk, seeking the consolations of true religion. He dismissed my response peremptorily and effectively put an end to argument by producing a pistol. 'You will come, minister, or that fine speech will be your last,' he threatened. 'I have horses waiting outside. The sooner you perform your duties, the sooner you will be back home.'

My terror was beyond words. My housekeeper urged me, 'Go with him, sir. He means to do exactly as he says.'

The good woman made my mind up. Possibly, in doing so, she saved my life. Now sadly departed this world, she was ever a true servant to me, but she held MacPhee in superstitious awe and later denied all memory of his having produced a gun, or of the advice she gave me, saying only that I had done the Christian thing in answering the bandit's request, and the least said about the incident the better.

It was a nightmare journey. In no time I was soaked to the skin. We left a decently surfaced military road for an old drove road through the mountains, a track so faint that it was hardly discoverable to myself, but MacPhee never faltered. A full four hours passed before we dismounted. I could hardly discern ground from sky, or sky from loch. But my travails were not yet over. MacPhee now indicated I should enter into a contrivance on the loch side. I had no confidence whatever as to its suitability as a vessel. MacPhee, realising I was at the limit of my physical endurance, simply plucked me from my mount and bundled me into the bottom of the rude coracle. Taking comfort from the fact that the early Christians had come to Scotland in similar crafts, I gave myself up to the wild man's keeping – and to the gentle mercy of our Lord.

It seemed to me no small miracle that we crossed safely over to the island. In the first light of dawn I made out the outline of some sort of cabin composed of wattle, mud and sods. Compared with MacPhee's habitation, the cells of the Culdees must be considered civilised. That anyone should live thus in such primitive conditions in the midst of the most civilised country the world has known is an abomination, romantic only to those who need not endure such privation.

Inside, a flame glowed at the centre of the construction and smoke filled the air in a most unhealthful manner. The place reeked of tallow. I leaned back on a heap of fleeces, utterly exhausted. MacPhee blew on the glowing peats, raising a weak flame. In the flickering light I observed that there was a third party in the dwelling, the slight figure of a young woman, with a shawl wrapped round her, obscuring her features. MacPhee took her hand in a gentle enough manner and led her over to me, saying, 'Come then, minister. Do what you have to, and wed us.'

Though I felt thoroughly overwhelmed, my first duty is to our Lord. I could not proceed without satisfying myself as to the willingness of the young woman to engage in marriage. Her prospective husband was much older than she and I suspected she might have been abducted to assuage his lust. I therefore summoned the courage to ask for leave to examine her. MacPhee consented. Though her English was imperfect, I established she had real admiration for MacPhee. She told me that her father had objected to the arrangement, causing them to elope. MacPhee had carried the girl on his back by dead of night over the mountains from the west, like an eagle stealing a chick from another bird's nest.

'How old are you, my lass?' I finally enquired.

She did not answer, but lowered her head. I enquired again, indicating that I must know, in order to formalise the religious ceremony. MacPhee replied, becoming angry again, that she was sixteen past Easter.

'Do you doubt my word?' he challenged me.

I was in no position to demand documentary proof, which in all probability was lacking. Besides, I felt that my Christian duty might best be served by gaining influence with MacPhee in obliging him and thus, possibly, effecting his moral rehabilitation. Further, I was aware of the dire situation of famine in the Rough Bounds. People there were starving, and in these circumstances MacPhee might well care for the poor girl better than her father – who was, in any case, most likely a Papist, for almost the entire populace of the Rough Bounds follows Rome, blind to the true revelation of our Lord, and deaf to all reason.

The sacrament of Christian marriage was then performed, in as strange a location as it ever can have been. Afterwards, MacPhee's wife prepared a marriage feast while he fortified my powers corporeal with a measure of whisky, which he proudly informed me was of his own making. It warmed my frozen bones and after partaking of some venison collops prepared over the fire, I lay on the rude pile of sheepskins occupying one corner of the cabin and was soon asleep. I awoke but once, roused by the sounds of the consummation of the marriage at which I had officiated.

Again under cover of darkness, Macphee escorted me back to the manse. The prospect of repose in my own bed, between clean sheets, made me desirous of quitting his company as quickly as possible. However, he dismounted after me and held out a sovereign, to 'cover the costs of marriage ceremony,' as he put it.

'I cannot take your money, MacPhee, for I know not whether it was honestly come by,' was my reply.

His pride seemed hurt. Pressing the coin into my hand he continued, 'This was earned by the sale of my own goats. Do not believe all that is said about me, minister. The labourer is worth his hire.'

I decided to accept, commenting that I hoped his encounter with the blessings of the Christian religion should not be his last.

Sadly, MacPhee's contacts with the Kirk remained as circumscribed as before and he continued on his wayward path. I made one further visit to his island refuge. This was not long before his recent capture, a full decade and half since our original meeting. This time our encounter was much less dramatic. I was bidding farewell to worshippers at the Kirk door when I noticed MacPhee, mounted on a nag and with another tied at its bridle, waiting at the wall of the glebe. While the curious hung around to watch, I went over to him.

'Well, Mr MacPhee, have you come at last to seek the benefits of religious doctrine?'

'I have come,' he replied brokenly, 'to ask if you will accompany me to bury my son.'

The man's grief was pitiable. I strove to persuade him to have the child buried in consecrated ground, but he cut short me with,

'He will be buried on my island, with or without your offices.'

I changed apparel before mounting the horse which, like MacPhee himself, had lost the sheen of youth. I endeavoured to engage MacPhee in conversation but he was unwilling to respond and so I left him to the consolation of his grief. The news of his tragedy had preceded us and as we passed, inhabitants of hovels by the roadside came out and respectfully removed their headgear. Higher into the mountains we climbed, until we had reached the place by the side of a loch where MacPhee's boat was hidden amongst scrub birk.

A most poignant scene greeted my eyes upon entering his dwelling. Mrs MacPhee and two little girls were weeping inconsolably. MacPhee informed me that the boy had drowned. The coffin had been crudely wrought with what materials came to hand. On its side I could discern the name of a well-known fish merchant, printed on the barrel staves used in the coffin's construction. I conducted the burial service, then MacPhee led his tragic entourage to an isolated spot where a hole had already been dug. There we interred the infant, to whom I promised eternal resurrection.

Despite their sorrow, the MacPhees had not neglected to prepare a simple funeral repast. While we were eating I enquired if they would like me to baptise the remaining children in the name of our Lord Jesus Christ. MacPhee did not offer the resistance I had expected, while his wife expressed strong approval. With great alacrity, I welcomed their progeny into the family of the Kirk. For these services MacPhee once more insisted on my accepting a coin, stating that he would accept charity from none.

He again accompanied me back to the manse. I suggested that for the sake of the remaining children he might wish to accept the visitations of a missionary from the Society for the Propagation of Christian Knowledge who could come to teach them the rudiments of education and properly verse them in Christian doctrine. MacPhee gruffly assented. I arranged for the missionary, Mr Barclay, to undertake this task; thereafter he often called in after his visits to Loch Quoich, to give me account of his work. The children had no slate and performed their writing in the sand by means of the quill feather of an eagle. Their father, himself illiterate, was inordinately proud of their progress. I was given to hope that the reformation at least of the children would be accomplished, and that they might be saved from following the errant path.

But dreadful outrages recently committed by MacPhee have dashed all such hopes. He is now incarcerated in the jail at Fort William where he is held with wife and children together in a bitterly cold cell. The good Doctor Kennedy, who was with the family when I arrived, fears that the girls show signs of cholera, which is rampant in the jail and in the town itself.

When the doctor had left, I entreated MacPhee to confess his crimes and show repentance, whereby he might find forgiveness in a future spiritual state – though he could hardly expect reprieve in this temporal one. He advanced the deluded argument that the court would find no one willing to testify against him, so that his eventual release was ensured. I was able to disabuse him of this, by informing him that Corriechoille and several of his servants had already signed affidavits against him and that now that he was no longer at large, others would been emboldened to bear witness in his case. This hardly troubled his countenance. He asserted that no jury in Lochaber would convict him of anything which could lead to the death penalty. I was heavy with the import of what I had to communicate to him.

'Mr MacPhee, things have come to a more desperate pass than that,' I said in level tones. I drew his attention to the capital charge against Mrs MacPhee, relating to the fire at the inn. Several witnesses had come forward to swear that not only did she deliberately set the inn ablaze, but that she fired into the building as people were attempting to flee, thus being the direct cause of the deaths which ensued.

The import of this struck home. MacPhee swore violent oaths in both English and Gaelic, insisting the accusations were false. I felt it better to let him expend his energies for a while in this manner, before resuming my own discourse. I conveyed to the prisoner the offer with which I had been charged.

'Whether or not these accusations be true, I cannot say. I can say, however, that there is evidence enough to convict Helen. I have been charged with the mission of assuring you that those who are the prime movers behind bringing you to trial will be willing to drop the charges against your unfortunate wife, on condition that you yourself plead guilty to the accusations levelled against you.'

Once again, he exploded in anger, this time as much against myself as against those on whose behalf I had spoken. I think that his overweening pride forbade him to plead guilty to actions he justified by circumstances. His parting remark was, 'I thank you for your concern, minister. But I owe you nothing for your services on this occasion.'

Any further attempt to persuade him in his present state of mind was useless, and so I left him to his cold cell and the colder comfort of his expectations, hoping that rational consideration of his situation would convince him that the course I had outlined was the only one open to him.

Here ends my deposition to the Kirk Session.

To conclude today's sermon, I wish to emphasise that this tragic story amply demonstrates that to step outside the law or take justice into our own hands, will yield bitter consequences. The civil authorities, like the Lord, must not be mocked. Any among you who have intelligence of wrong-doing perpetrated by MacPhee must overcome the temptation to keep it to yourselves. Any among you who are called to perform jury service must do so, with all honesty, in obedience to the majesty of the law. In this wicked and imperfect world, we must render unto Caesar what belongs to Caesar. Take care lest, like the unfortunate MacPhee, you are tempted onto the path that leads to eternal damnation in the sight of the Lord.

Amen.

The Sheriff

Ardlui, the 25th May, 1850

I would have had him hanged the first time. It would have saved this journey to have him hanged now.

I had become weary of the Highland circuit with which I was engaged as a young sheriff. Formerly, I relished the novelty of escaping the Edinburgh law courts and offices, of touring the country and ridding it of its rascals and parasites. The consciousness of serving improvement, of bringing law and respect for property to these recently-barbarous lands, did not wane with time. But my ability to withstand the rigours of the climate and to endure the lack of material refinements declined with age. My legal practice in Edinburgh so absorbed my energies that I had almost forgotten MacPhee.

Then I heard that he had been taken, again. Despite all his cunning and his seemingly charmed existence, he has been taken.

A colleague from another legal practice, with which my own is well-connected, has the current incumbency of the Western Circuit. I had in the past done this firm some favour... suffice to say, I used my influence to arrange to take the place of the intended judge in MacPhee's case. My desire to complete the unfinished business of almost three decades overcame any reluctance to make a trip into the mountains. To rid the country of that canker who was MacPhee would undoubtedly be a fine work.

Curious to observe the changes in the Highlands, I resolved to make some of my journey overland, rather than take the steamer direct from the Broomielaw to Fort William. As I sat in the train from Edinburgh to Glasgow, I recalled how the same journey had involved an interminably slow passage on a canal boat on the previous occasion I went to hang MacPhee. In a little over an hour I reached the western metropolis and took the fine road to Loch Lomond pier, where I boarded the steamer that would take me part of my way. The scene from the deck was really magnificent as it passed through the islands it serves with mail and supplies and headed northwards underneath the mountain called Lomond. I lunched with the other passengers, most of whom were voyaging for pleasure – tourists, as they are now called. This frivolous sort gape at the landscape without the least reflection on the drain the Highlands represents to the national economy. The backwardness of the region is much to do with the congenital indolence of the chronically backward-looking Gael, whose character the superficial mind finds romantic or picturesque.

There is a trend these days, begun in my opinion by the writings of Sir Walter Scott, for Scotland to be seen as a genus of Celtic nation, with the attendant tartan, pipes and other such Highland bric à brac. Sadly, this view appears to be shared by our present monarch, who has acquired a Highland estate wherein to indulge such fancies. The truth is that it is the more prosaic Saxon element which has been the fount of all that is worthwhile in our national character, of religion, science and progress in general; the Celtic element represents the peripheral and the barbaric.

The steamer itself is named after Rob Roy, a freebooting

scoundrel who in no way deserves the elevation to a figure of romantic myth. Rob Roy was a miscreant who would himself have hung, had there been the efficient exercise of justice in the glens and bens in his day. But the rule of law is there today, as Ewan MacPhee will find out ere long.

I had sent advance notice of my arrival, yet there was no one waiting for me at the pier at the north end of the loch. I asked an old man mending a boat in which direction the hostelry lay. After some pretence that he did not understand, and responses in Gaelic, a coin produced a remarkable increase in his linguistic abilities and he directed me the quarter mile or so to the hotel. But neither bribe nor entreaty would persuade him to carry my valise; ignorant though these peasants are, they still deem themselves too high-born for such a task. I regretted my initial generosity. A lesser token might have produced a greater compliance in pursuit of further emolument. This indeed is the lesson to be applied hereabouts, that to be cruel is ultimately to be kind.

The inn was a wretched place, though classed as a fine house hereabouts, where slates and dressed stone are enough to give airs to a building and its occupants. At least it is warm, though cleanliness would be too much to ask of people who hold that washing is unhealthy. My desire to have some heated water in my chamber caused consternation. The water was at least clean, if lukewarm; prior experience had prepared me to bring my own towel and soap.

I indicated to the landlord that I would sup in my room, as I had work to do on the brief. Over the next hour or two, items of my repast, in no regular order, arrived at my door, brought by a slatternly maid who appeared to be both deaf and dumb. Tea came first. Milk and sugar for it, in a pot never cleaned since Creation, came a while later. A fine grilled trout arrived, but its accompanying potatoes were delayed and arrived cold. Bread was finally brought as I prepared to retire; it was stale and I laid it aside, not before noticing finger prints in the butter.

The slattern came to clear the dishes, which she laid outside in the corridor, then returned. I looked at her curiously and realised that behind the dirt and tatters she was a decently-formed specimen of her sex. I am familiar with the methods by which serving maids supplement their incomes and was little surprised when she began to loosen her bodice and kick off her shoes preparatory to disrobing. Anticipating a long day the morrow, I was in no mood to prolong her stay. I indicated she should adjust her dress and opened the door, pointing to the dishes she was meant to clear. She left me to my repose.

Inveroran, the 26th May, 1850

I had hoped to have progressed further on the road to Fort William today, in order to have a full day there to prepare for the legal proceedings. Events however, dictated otherwise. Perhaps it is no great loss, for I have enjoyed a pleasant and instructive day. This hostelry, an improvement on last night's accommodation, is situated in a most picturesque spot by a lake. To the south lies an extensive forest of pine woods, of great antiquity.

The delay was caused by the failure of the coach service, which normally runs three days a week, to run on this particular day, leading to the necessity of hiring horses and a guide, no small task in these parts. Knowing the difficulty of dealing with the indigenous peasantry, I instructed my landlord to procure me what I needed, indicating the maximum price I was willing to pay – but knowing I would probably have to pay more. This rigmarole went on most of the morning. Before noon, a man was found to accompany me. He was in as poor shape as his ponies – horses is too grand a description of the beasts. Thankfully, he claimed to have little English and left me to my own thoughts until it was time for him to head back. Despite the fact his paltry labour had procured him more than he could normally expect to earn in a month, he took the money without thanks and asked – he who had claimed not to be able to use other than his primitive Gaelic tongue – 'Are you the man that is to hang that poor body, MacPhee?'

I expressed my annoyance at his arrogant presumption, and bade him be gone. But he persisted: 'He is an old man, who should be let die in peace. May fortune not favour your work.'

This unpleasantness somewhat marred the day. The weather was fair and the road, being one of those constructed by the military a century ago in the initial stages of their pacification of the country, was of reasonable quality. I noticed that several areas the aboriginal woods which have stood useless for generations have recently been felled, allowing the sturdy sheep to graze on these previously unutilised hillsides. Apparently sheep do not bring their former yields and that some proprietors have turned their estates over to hunting, though I am sure such schemes must carry great risks. It strikes me as imperative to open these valleys by extending the railways: if this engineering achievement proves feasible, it will introduce the benefits of industry and necessary habits of diligence to these northern lands.

We journeyed through the upper reaches of Glen Falloch, enjoying the occasional vista of a fine waterfall. An acquaintance had provided me with a letter of introduction to Mr Grey, the manager of the lead manufactory at Tyndrum, where we arrived around mid-afternoon. His substantial residence was surrounded by trees set back from a clutter of low slung miners' rows by the burn. Mr Grey asked me to join him for tea with another guest, the Reverend Mackenzie of the Society for the Propagating of Christian Knowledge. The hour I spent with these gentlemen was in pleasant contrast to that spent with my recalcitrant equerry. Mr Mackenzie, who was introduced to me as a scholar in the Gaelic language, instills the rudiments of English and arithmetic into the local children during the winter months In his missionary work of promoting sound Christian learning he has a hard furrow to plough: the gentry hereabouts have episcopal leanings and as for the peasants, their conception of the doctrine of our Lord Jesus is still heavily intermixed with residual pagan practices – and this in an area where St Fillan, one of the earliest Columban missionaries, brought the blessed light of salvation over a thousand years ago!

Mr Grey is a reserved Englishman, impressively well versed in the scientific aspects of lead mining. The hills above the house are zig-zagged with miners' tracks. But his manufactory just outside the village lies idle. Mr Grey is reasonably sanguine, anticipating an upturn in demand for pipes and gutters. His pessimism regarding the long-term possibilities economic prospects for lead mining in this area has more to do with the attitude of the local labourers. They are prepared to work to acquire some item, then they halt, having no desire to save money. The hills abound with easily poached game and fish and illicit distilling is commonplace. Mr Grey was gratified to learn of my purpose in travelling northwards. I suggested that those who refused to engage in permanent labour should be evicted from their houses, but he said the problem would then be that no one from outside the Highlands would wish to come to work at Tyndrum.

At that point, Reverend Mackenzie observed, rather inappropriately, that since the workers were laid off without pay when trade was slack, they saw no obligation to undertake to work if it did not suit them. I suggested that he might do well to explain the relative duties of capital and labour to his congregation. I can only hope that he sees fit to take my point.

Refreshed by our conversation, I resumed my journey, arriving at my present accommodation in time to accept the landlord's cordial invitation to sup with him. For a Highlander, he is a man of some education. He formerly worked in the calico printing industry in Glasgow and saved enough money to invest in his present enterprise. Unusually for innkeepers hereabouts, he understands the basics of diligence and cleanliness. Though his establishment is relatively Spartan, by Highlands standards it very well-provided. My host is a great admirer of a Gaelic poet who formerly lived in these parts and, though illiterate, he could recite all his verses to the number of 70,000 lines. It strikes me that the energies of both poet and innkeeper might have been devoted to a more useful pursuit.

Kinlochleven, the 27th May, 1850

This morning I again had bother procuring horses. The population here is sparse and none was prepared to provide horses or cross Rannoch Moor with me. Eventually my landlord sent an urchin to the factor's house some distance away and an hour or so later the good man himself came with two animals of decent quality, and offered to guide me, but only as far as Kingshouse, as he needs be back with the horses on the morrow. Mr Mackerachar proved a most agreeable companion. He refused all payment for the hire of the horses, saying that his master, the estate owner, would have performed the service himself, had he been here to do so. He explained that my difficulty in finding a horse was because my purpose was known throughout the country. Even in this area, where MacPhee has never set foot, his fame is widespread. In his work as a factor, Mackerachar encountered opposition to every project for improvement, the peasantry preferring to remain in their ignorant and bigoted ways. We crossed the dreary wastes of Rannoch Moor, passing only the odd drover with a cluster of cattle. I found the Kingshouse to be a well-appointed staging inn, with livery and guides, and I set out with confidence on the next stage of my journey. The new parliamentary road goes through Glencoe but the direct route is over the Devil's Staircase, a steep section of the old military road which climbs the ridge behind the hotel. From the summit of the pass I surveyed a scene of barely imaginable grandeur and savagery, sharply delineated in the late afternoon light. Behind me lay the jagged peaks of Glencoe itself, apparently never trodden by man, and unlikely ever to be so. One can see why the Highlander is reluctant to leave this land. But these sentiments do not recognize the economic realities that now prevail.

At Kinlochleven I found accommodation with the local doctor, to whom I was directed from the local inn, which was fully occupied by a party of drovers. The doctor is a misanthropic man who accommodates me more from duty than pleasure. He tells me there is cholera in Fort William. As I was weary and he uncommunicative, I retired early.

Ft William, the 28th May, 1850

Seldom can a day, begun with such fair prospects, have ended in such frustration. The weather was utterly foul. I had a miserable journey through a dreary glen to Fort William, a town largely composed of thatched hovels. There are, however, some fine stone buildings including a bank, churches and two decent hotels which would not disgrace Glasgow or Edinburgh. I took accommodation in one of these and enjoyed my first bath since leaving Edinburgh. After a substantial meal, I was in considerably better humour.

My mind turned once more to MacPhee, who I would imminently encounter. I was confident he could not cheat justice this time; the charges of desertion, kidnapping and murder are each enough to convict him and have him hang, even if he has the folly to plead not guilty and force a full trial. I expect him to plead guilty in return for the charges against his wife being dropped.

Misplaced delicacy of feeling amongst juries has been known to lead to the substitution of transportation for life for the capital charge, in order to secure conviction. I myself steadfastly resisted this practice. Our overseas possessions are better stocked by the law-abiding, than by the dregs such as MacPhee.

After dinner the rain eased off and I walked over to the jail. I could not suppress an impatient desire to see the prisoner. The jail stands in the grounds of the old Fort itself, whose policies have become the town's graveyard.

The jailer greeted me with respect, but seemed ill at ease. I asked to see the cell where the bandit was confined.

'Aye, the cell he *was* in,' repeated the jailer with an emphasis which provoked a sinister sense of foreboding.

I was led past the old jail, a rough stone and turf construction where prisoners were held together without regard to sex or crime, and into a new block, with separate cells and hygienic facilities.

'The prisoners preferred the old prison,' observed my guide, 'they say it was far warmer.' His next statement was pronounced quite casually, as if he were unaware that its import destroyed the *raison d'être* of my being there: 'This was MacPhee's cell. He died two days ago of the cholera. His whole family died last week. The doctor who treated them died of the disease too. He is being buried now.'

I walked outside to the burial ground. A small crowd of the better class of persons stood by a grave in which a fine wooden coffin had been laid, and at the head of which stood a chiselled memorial stone. I raised my hat in respect as I passed the mourners. At the lower end of the cemetery was a much larger crowd, of the meaner sort, around a grave where I deduced Macphee must lie. They made aside for me as I approached, and the grave digger halted in his work of throwing quicklime on the body lying in a common trench where the bandit's wife and children had been previously interred, as I could discern from body parts emerging through the soil beneath his corpse. I looked at MacPhee's face, awaiting the dissolution of the lime, and imagined a rictal sneer in his return gaze. He had escaped justice again, this time forever.

I lifted a clod from the ground, and dropped it into the grave of the man who had defeated me.

Author's Afterword

AS MUCH AS MANY BETTER KNOWN primitive rebels such as Rob Roy MacGregor, Ewan MacPhee is a fascinating character, our last bandit – indeed last outlaw against whom any man's hand could be violently turned – and one whose life-struggles reached epic, almost mythical proportions and ended in tragedy.

By MacPhee's day, traditional Highland society had been all but destroyed and the Clearances were at their height. He lived a century after the Jacobite Rebellions in an age of scientific revolution, technological advance and the birth of modern political theories. In this respect, MacPhee fits into the pattern described by EJ Hobsbawm in his book *Bandits* (1969): 'Social banditry occurs in all types of human society which lie between tribal and kinship organisations, and modern capitalist and industrial society, (including the transition to agrarian capitalism)'.

I first came across a reference to Ewan MacPhee in Alexander MacDonald's *Story and Song from Loch Ness-Side*, 1914, re-issued by the Gaelic Society of Inverness in 1982. That Ewan MacPhee remained a hardly known local hero a century and a half after his death astonished me and my fascination with him stimulated further investigations into his life.

Edward Ellice was a Glenquoich landowner, whose grandfather had known MacPhee and passed down stories of the outlaw, which were reprinted in the wonderful book *Place-Names in Glengarry and Glenquoich*, 1898. James Logan's re-issue in 1900 of MacIan's *Highlanders at Home*, added some more information, as well as giving a portrait of MacPhee and his family painted by MacIan himself for the original 1843 edition. More snippets about MacPhee's dramatic exploits were gleaned from newspapers, including the *Inverness Courier* of the 1840s; I made the unlikely discovery of a reference to MacPhee in the *Scottish Mountaineering Club Journal* of the 1920s: in an article detailing ascents of peaks in the wild west, the Reverend Burn recounted several stories about MacPhee which he had heard at Lochaber firesides in the early years of the twentieth century. Some detail on MacPhee's conflict with Corriechoille appeared in *Antiquarian Notes* (second series) 1897, by Charles Fraser-Mackintosh.

In 1995 I wrote an article for the *West Highland Free Press*, recounting the few details of MacPhee's life that were reasonably certain. He was born, possibly at Corrie Bhuie in Glen Quoich, around 1784, and he died in 1850 in Fort William (though one report has Fort Augustus). He was enrolled in the military by his landowner, MacDonnel of Glengarry – seemingly against his will – about 1808, and saw service in the Napoleonic wars. He deserted his unit, a capital offence in wartime, and for a while was sequestered with his mother at a place in Lochaber called Fedden. He was captured in the early 1820s, but escaped in dramatic fashion, to live in the wilds of Glen Quoich, on Eilean MhicPhee, an island which acquired his name in local lore – and on Ordnance Survey maps. It was flooded by hydro-electric workings in the 1950s

There he built a cabin and raised a family with a Knoydart woman he is reputed to have abducted. Various crimes, many of a capital nature, were attributed to him – crimes which were neither proven nor disproven, since MacPhee was never brought to trial. In the 1840s he came into conflict with Cameron of Corriechoille, a sheep drover who was extending his empire throughout the wilderness of west Lochaber; MacPhee's struggle with Cameron led to his imprisonment. He died in prison while awaiting trial. Had it been held, the trial would have furnished data invaluable to future biographical studies. Literary references to MacPhee are few and many tales associated with him were lost with the demise of the oral tradition in the Highlands. However, MacPhee would not let me alone, and kept preying on my imagination. I wanted to flesh out the bones of his story and through it convey something of the social transformations taking place in the Highlands of his day; the book in your hands is the result.

My dozen or so characters, some real, some invented, describe the bandit's impact upon them; having created a fictional 'editor', DG Place, I selected incidents from Highland folklore which fall within the bounds of historical credibility. Like Scott's method in composing his *Rob Roy*, I have recorded faithfully certain materials I found concerning the Loch Quoich bandit, stretched others to the limits, and supplied some from my own invention. Unravelling the skein of faction may be an attraction of the book, but my objective was not to provide a conundrum but a compendium of tales which do some justice to the memory of Ewan MacPhee.

Ian R Mitchell, Glasgow, May, 2003

Glossary

birk	birch
bocan	a ghost which takes different forms
bodach Caonich	old man of Caonich
cailleach	old woman
clachan	township
erne	sea eagle
Erse	Gaelic
Gaidhealtachd	Gaelic world
Gall	strangers (non Gaels)
garron	small work horse
gauger	exciseman
ghillie	servant on a hunt
gralloch	gut (v)
kebbuck	hunk of cheese
lus an laoigh	club moss
Monzie	French
mucan beag	little pig
Muick	place of the pigs
poll nan con	pool of the dogs
Sasunnach	English
Sasunnaich	English (pl)
sheltie	pony
tarbh-uisge	water bull, water horse
tocher	dowry
usquebaugh	whisky